Books by Nancy Hale

THE YOUNG DIE GOOD

NEVER ANY MORE

THE EARLIEST DREAMS

THE PRODIGAL WOMEN

BETWEEN THE DARK AND THE DAYLIGHT

THE SIGN OF JONAH

THE EMPRESS'S RING

HEAVEN AND HARDPAN FARM

A NEW ENGLAND GIRLHOOD

A New England Girlhood

A New England Girlhood

by NANCY HALE

Little, Brown and Company

Boston   Toronto

LIBRARY OF CONGRESS CATALOG CARD NO. 58-7869

FIRST EDITION

Chapter 8 is reprinted from THE EMPRESS's RING by Nancy Hale (© copyright 1955 by Nancy Hale) by permission of Charles Scribner's Sons. Chapter 19 is reprinted by permission of *Harper's Bazaar*. All but Chapters 8, 12 and 19 appeared in the *New Yorker*.

Published simultaneously in Canada
by Little, Brown & Company (Canada) Limited

PRINTED IN THE UNITED STATES OF AMERICA

To Fredson Bowers

Introduction

IN 1892 A SERIES OF ARTICLES BY EDWARD EVERETT
Hale appeared in the *Atlantic Monthly* which were published in book form the following year under the title *A
New England Boyhood*. In an introduction added for
the 1899 edition, the author, who was my grandfather,
tells how Horace Scudder, the editor of the *Atlantic*, had
suggested to him that he emulate the example of his
kinswoman Lucy Larcom, who had published her recollections under the title *A New England Girlhood*, and
recall to memory the already nearly mythical years when
Boston was the only city in New England except Ver-
gennes, Vermont; Hartford, Connecticut; and York,
Maine. More than half a century later I am venturing,
with the present volume, to vary once again what might
almost seem to be a family title.

A New England Boyhood covered the years between
Hale's birth in 1822 and his entering Harvard at the
age of thirteen — not an extraordinary age for college at
the time; his uncle, Edward Everett, had done the same

twenty years before. Everett's sister, Sarah Preston Everett, had married Nathan Hale, nephew of the patriot, and was the mother of the eight Hale children. (There is a family story, to illustrate how tiny Boston was then, that after my great-grandmother's marriage and removal to Boston, a girlhood friend from Dorchester walked along Tremont Street, asking everyone she met, "Can you tell me where she that was Sally Everett lives?" and received directions on her third try.)

Familiar links connect my grandfather's childhood with my own. Nathan Hale was editor of the Boston *Daily Advertiser* and president of the first type foundry in New England. His sons grew up knowing how to set type and arrange it. Two family newspapers were composed and edited by the Hale children: the *New England Herald* by the older two, and the *Public Informer,* the latter title wickedly suggested by grownups to the littler ones, among them Lucretia, who, when she grew up, wrote *The Peterkin Papers.* Under ideal conditions these journals appeared on the breakfast table on alternate Mondays. I am told that when I was about to turn eight years old, my mother reported in some astonishment to my father — who was one of Hale's nine children — that I seemed to think I wanted a printing press for my birthday. "Don't be alarmed," he is supposed to have said. "All Hale children ask for printing presses when they are eight." With the small press I got, I used to put out a family newspaper at wildly irregular intervals, called the *Society Cat*.

A New England Boyhood contains much to surprise and entertain those interested in old Boston. There is that character and tyrant Fullum, a male domestic who also gardened, carpentered, cared for horses, and, although he could barely read and write, was regarded by two generations of little Hale boys as omniscient and omnipotent. He had worked for the Websters before coming to the Hales when Mr. Webster entered Congress in the fall of 1820. Born in 1790, Fullum became by the time of his death in 1886 the last representative, in a Hibernianized Boston, of the Yankee hired man.

Hale rescues from oblivion the Wishing Stone on Boston Common, which was one of the boulders blasted to make the curbstone of the Frog Pond in 1823. The stone stood a little east of the foot of Walnut Street; if you went round it backward nine times and repeated the Lord's Prayer backward, whatever you wished would come to pass.

Hale was one of the first four pupils in Lorenzo Papanti's famous dancing classes, where Signor Papanti taught the children their steps while playing music to dance to on the violin tucked under his chin. Hale remembers old taverns (never called inns) such as the Indian Queen in Bromfield Street, the Bunch of Grapes in State Street, the Lamb, the Lion, and the Lafayette, all with appropriately painted signs swinging out in front. They were small, he recalls, but quite large enough for their needs: Nathan Hale, who was considered a fanatic as a railroad prophet and later became the first president of the Boston and Worcester Railway, in about 1832 made at Faneuil Hall the extravagant prediction that as many as nine travelers would come daily from Springfield to Boston if the trip could be reduced to five hours. When the Hales went to Cape Ann for a holiday, it took them two days to get there, with Fullum driving them in a hired barouche. (Fullum arranged a duplicate set of reins, attached not to the bits but to the rings on the pads, for the use of the youngest boy.) "What is it?" cried the fishermen's children in those remote parts, lining up as the carriage passed and "making their manners" — bowing, not in deference but in salutation. "It ain't the mail, and it ain't a shay!"

Marlborough pie, unknown today, was to be found on Boston dinner tables, and invariably at Thanksgiving. Every old and well-regulated New England family had its own traditional method of making this delicacy, which was filled with a mixture of lemon and apple; I remember my own father reminiscing about the wonders of Marlborough pie. Speaking of the feast of Thanksgiving, Hale remarks, "Christmas, as a holiday of this sort, was absolutely unknown in this Puritan family." Puritan families, whether Unitarian or Evangelical, spoke of "going to meeting"; but Hale adds that in Boston, unlike the country, the buildings themselves were always called churches. The Puritan theory was that the family is the church, and the father of the family a priest competent to carry on worship at home, which he did morning and evening. Evening service anywhere else was considered an innovation; and when "the Connecticut religion" was introduced into Boston by the building of Park Street Church and the arrival to preach in it of Lyman Beecher (whose granddaughter Hale married), the interior arrangements for lighting up the church seemed heresy to the old Puritans.

Among much else that has altered diametrically between that day and this, nothing is more striking than the attitude toward the past to which my grandfather subscribed. In every line of his reminiscences there breathes the assumption that the past is something which will stay firmly behind, instead of a force that may throw its light forward to color the future. Hale (who originated the Unitarian slogan "Look up and not down; look out and not in; look forward and not backward") takes it for granted that it is possible to draw a clear dividing line at a point called the present, over which the past can be trusted never to encroach. Past, present, future are for him three entirely separate domains.

His attitude to the past was in direct relation to his attitude toward the future. William James, in his *Varieties of Religious Experience,* cites Hale as an exemplar of "the religion of healthy-mindedness" or "the once-born man." He quotes him as saying, "I can remember that when I was coming to manhood, the half-philosophical novels of the time had a deal to say about young men and maidens who were facing 'the problem of life.' I had no idea what the problem of life was. To live with all my might seemed to me easy; to learn where there was so much to learn seemed pleasant and almost of course; to lend a hand, if one had a chance, natural; and if one did this, why, he enjoyed life because he could not help it, and without proving to himself that he ought to enjoy it." Such an enviable philosophy might account for the cheerful obedience with which, in *A New England Boyhood*, what is past lies down and stays down. What is over is considered only from an antiquarian point of view. Hale was, indeed, a great antiquarian. In all his books he demonstrates his vast ability to remember things other people forgot. But, in gazing into the still waters of the past, he seems always to have left what lay at the bottom untroubled.

Not that he fancied memory to be a trustworthy reporter. In a foreword to the 1900 edition of *A New England Boyhood*, he writes, "After a man has written an autobiography, you might catch him again, when he did not remember much of it, and he would write another, quite as entertaining but quite different from the first." But though his memory of it might be unreliable, it was possible for Hale to stand, in looking back over his long life, as though on the apex of a great pyramid, gazing down its gently sloping sides.

I do not think that such an attitude toward the past is possible to someone writing reminiscently today. Speculation about the unity of time, up to and through the nineteenth century, was easily avoidable; today, after Proust and Joyce, after Freud and Jung, in the subjective realm, at least, we shall never be able to avoid it again. Instead of a secure pyramid, the past looks to us more like a sea in which we are suspended, float, move minutely, as though a sailboat. Above arches the sky, or future. Only the faintest variation in shades of blue and pearl differentiates it from water at the horizon. Or we see the past as the river that runs beside a man who is building something out of stones which will take some part of the future to finish: a wall, a house. He turns and peers down into the blue stream flowing past him; then he reaches into the water and brings up the stone he needs. Having once perceived that in looking into the past we can see a reflection of the future, that in regarding environment we face a looking glass, we will never again be able to believe in the old trichotomy. The boundaries are down, the whole territory is seen to be one, with time only the self caught in the act of measuring itself against passing events.

There is a difference of intent between my grandfather's pieces about his childhood and the pieces about mine here collected from the past twenty-five years of writing. His were designedly factual and mine were never meant to be. The varied settings in time, in place, given to the same summer-resort scene in Chapters 6 and 21 illustrate the protean uses to which I have put the past. And I did not, moreover, own a ring that once belonged to the Empress of Austria; the ring I did own, which looked something like the one in Chapter 3, I never lost. Things did get lost; and that I was not the only child to lose and mourn something indefinably precious was demonstrated to me by such letters as the one from a man in Canada, who said, "I too lost something, when I was six — the little pearl-handled knife my father had given me. I know how you felt about losing your ring, and I know you are only calling it a ring."

My pieces, although their background is the scenery and characters that bounded my childhood, are intended less to be about the real and ascertainable past than about my memory of it; and memory, as a mode of thinking, tends to burst spontaneously into fantasy at every turn. Some of the events in the stories are true to fact, some not. What interested me in writing them was to try to catch the reverberations from childhood that sometimes make it seem as if the first few years of all our lives constitute a riddle which it is a lifework to solve.

A New England Girlhood

1

Of the house where we lived until i was four I can remember only certain effects of light, but I can remember it very well in terms of where the light came in. It is as if those infant years were lived in a dark box with holes cut in it; the holes, the arrangement of the holes, what I saw outside the holes are all that remains.

For example, I can remember my grandfather, who died when I was not quite three, as an immense shape filling the oblong of the front door. I am part way down a flight of stairs; my mother stands at the bottom opening the door; but we are shadowy and I feel rather than see us. What I am looking at is that huge silhouette — he was six feet four — against the outdoor sunshine of the porch, the path, the garden.

It is the same with my nursery. I lie in my crib in the left-hand rear corner of the dark cube; there are two windows, rectangles of light that fades and is brought up again. One window is on the left-hand wall and the other is straight ahead of me. Somebody comes and picks

3

me up in his arms and carries me to the left-hand window. Is it my father?

My father was a witty man, with his own sense of humor. Years later, at the end of the first World War, we watched the victory march of the Yankee Division from the windows of an apartment at the corner of Beacon Street and Charles, where the parade was to start. A good many people were invited to sit by these windows, and I think I was the only child. As the parade began, the thrilling moment when General Edwards's horse stepped proudly forward across the line in front of the orderly ranks of the troops, a young mother who was one of our company began to berate herself for not having brought her six-month-old baby, so that she could hold him up to the unforgettable sight.

"He's too young to remember it," someone consoled her.

"But I could have told him later, 'You saw the parade of the returning Yankee Division,'" she insisted.

"Never mind," my father said. "You can tell him he saw it anyway."

My father used to pick me up from my crib in that dim, forgotten room and carry me to the left-hand window. It is dark outside, but not the darkness of indoors — a luminous dark. Far away across the fields shine hundreds of lights, white and twinkling and incandescent. "Look," my father says. "See the stars."

Only, in point of fact, they were not the stars. I am sure that he must have sometimes shown me the real

4

stars in the sky, but it was a family joke as I grew up that, held in my father's arms at the window looking east, I had pointed to the lights of Readville, a nearby slummy mill town, and said, only in baby talk, "Stars." He had preferred not to contradict me, and had continued to call my attention on other nights to these other stars. "The Readville stars" — it was a family byword. (When I was sixteen and went to stay at a New York hotel with my mother, she walked over to the window the night we arrived and stood looking down the length of Park Avenue. "What are you looking at?" I asked as I unpacked my bag at the back of the room. "The Readville stars," she said. It means anything shining, exciting, glamorous.)

Then I was four, and we moved to another house. I remember the first night there. I am eating my supper at the child-size table, in my new nursery; there is a piece of clean white oilcloth tacked over the black tabletop, making it quite new. My new wallpaper is blue, with little white lozenges in a pattern. Beside me in the wall is something I have never seen before — a black iron grillwork through which comes heat. It is a register. It is as though in that move from one house to another, in one day, the focus had shifted entirely. I am looking at the inside of my room for the first time. It is as if the lights had gone on, *inside* the house.

I grew up and left home and went to work. In my early twenties, I went to Italy for a time. It was the era of Mussolini. His stenciled silhouette, that jowly *profil perdu,* was on every hoarding, every stucco wall. But of politics I knew nothing and cared less, and I had been given a black silk shirt by a *commendatore* beau, and gone dancing in Florence with a Fascist Milanese of exalted lineage, and walked along the Lungarno by moonlight with an admirer who, as he passed acquaintances, exchanged the straight-armed Roman salute. *Giovanezza!* I was full of *giovanezza* and excitement as I was driven in a hired Fiat from Siena to Rome. We passed rosy hill towns out of medieval woodcuts as we sped along, and white oxen with horns six feet from tip to tip. To one side, across the romantic countryside, a ruined castle would appear suddenly. My driver spoke no English and I only the most rudimentary Italian, so we drove in silence. I was busy being in love with Italy. What a place! I planned how I would have a cap made of black felt, with a black silk tassel falling over one eye, to wear with my trophy black shirt. They would look very smart with a gray tailored suit.

The twilight deepened as we drove, and night fell, and then, as we rounded a curve or mounted a rise, I saw stretched before us a million faraway lights, shining in the dusk.

Stars, I thought in my intoxication; the blaze of stars.

My driver turned his head slightly and spoke out of the corner of his mouth.

"*E Roma,*" he said.

Now it is years later, and I live in a house that has no view at all, since our Virginia town is set in a cup in the mountains, and all the stars that can be seen are the real stars directly overhead. However, the inside of my house is charming to look at — dark-green walls downstairs, with white woodwork, and upstairs, lighter colors. In one bedroom I have a blue paper that reminds me of the paper in my old nursery, in that second house — the first room I ever really looked at.

But it made me sad the other day when, as I was remembering those things, I recognized that youthful blindness that could be so dazzled by a black shirt, so light-struck by Rome at dusk. I was, in fact, depressed; it gave me an uneasy feeling that I might still, at my age, be thrilling to some spectacle that was, really, only Readville stars. I must confess that I worried about it; I searched myself — oh, for several days.

But as one grows older, one learns not to allow oneself to become depressed. Activity is the cure. I invited several people to lunch, several people to dinner. The table looked lovely. I was quite overwhelmed by compliments on the food. Mrs. Harbridge asked me to head a committee to investigate local fiscal policies; Mr. Jameson asked me to be his assistant in the Blood Bank work. I had no idea people thought so highly of me. It was most gratifying. So that today, far from being depressed, I feel just fine, in the swim, definitely set up. Almost, I might say, excited.

7

2

THE THING, THE SPARK, THAT SET IN MOTION THE train of events that led to my present impossible situation was the experience of beginning to see those little pails and shovels in the windows of shops. Queer shops to see them in, always; don't get the idea I was visiting by the seaside when I saw them, or in a place likely to involve beach paraphernalia. No, it was always in our mountain-locked Virginia town that I saw them, or somewhere equally far from salt air: Richmond, or Raleigh, North Carolina. Yet there they sat in the shopwindows while I stood outside staring with that leap in my heart, almost like a heart attack: the classic, eternal pail-and-shovel set — a tin pail painted with nursery or circus figures and, accompanying it, a small tin shovel painted bright shiny red.

They stood out from their surroundings — newsstand stationery supplies, usually, or children's toys — with a vibrant and fateful significance. It's hard to explain how much they meant to me — I was so astonished at it myself. That pail — round, jolly, and meant for containing marvels; that shovel with its miraculously shiny red paint, latent with joy and possibilities. I would stand staring at them, my heart still skipping beats, while slowly over me crept the mood that they induced, boundlessly confident, self-contained, rakish, piratical — the mood, I realized after a bit, in which thirty, oh, thirty-five, years ago I used to proceed in triumph of a morning down the beach at Cod Harbor. In those days I would have been dressed in pink cotton rompers and an enormous straw hat as I carried my unspeakably potent pail and shovel, and accompanied by my mother in a long white linen dress and a hat trimmed with a chiffon veil. All those things are gone now; but the feeling — at once smug, daring, and as private as a tightly sealed clam — that a pail and shovel for digging on the beach used to give me lived on, apparently unmodified, as strong and buccaneerish as ever. This feeling, when I looked at a child's tin pail and shovel in the shopwindow of a hot, muggy, dusty Southern town miles from the sea, had nothing whatever to do with nostalgia, the sharp, yearning, sweet sensation that is weakness; this was a do-and-dare feeling, an up-and-at-'em feeling, strong and tough and secretive, and I suppose it is this feeling that, in the end, led to my present predicament.

At first, when I began to notice, so vividly, this anomaly, the pail and shovel in Southern shopwindows, I felt almost as if there were something queer about it, something, well, psychic. I must repeat that beach toys in such windows as those seemed as much fantasy as a surrealist landscape. Were the pail and shovel, I even asked myself, really there? Of course they were; and when I finally got myself to the point of asking my husband, in a manner studiedly casual, why such things should exist in inland shops, he replied with his usual painstaking patience at stupidity that they were doubtless for use in children's sand piles. I had never thought of that; instead, I had thought only of Cod Harbor, back in the days when I was a little girl in New England and we used to visit my Aunt Ellen at her house, The Barnacles.

In those days we traveled by train. As we jolted, jerked, bucketed along, I sat beside my mother, on the gritty red plush seat, with the window open because the weather was so hot. Blasts as from an oven came in the window, laden with cinders from the engine. My mother kept her veil down. Sometimes I would get a cinder in my eye; then the rite was always the same: "Close your eyes, darling. Don't rub them. Lift the lid by the eyelashes with your fingers and let it slide up against your lower lid. It'll come out." But mostly my mother leaned back against the plush seat back, exhausted. Summer at home meant gardening, pickling, preserving, canning — great boxes of strawberries or of tomatoes waiting on the wooden board over the set tubs for their turn to be plunged into the caldron of scalding water that my mother stood over with flushed cheeks and anxious brow — besides the incessant household duties of all year round — the fatiguing perfectionism of entertaining, the inadequate Irish servant girls, the unceasing effort to come up to a rigid standard that was so real that even I, at six, could feel it, like a presence behind an arras.

But now all was to be different, I knew, she knew; we were on the train for Cod Harbor. With each mile the atmosphere grew lighter, bluer; and when the conductor flung open the door at the end of the car and called out "Say — *lum! Say* — lum," a burst of new air, cool air, air vibrant with the smell of salt, came to us, and our vacation had begun.

We rode to the end of the line. At Harborport we descended the steps of the train into another world, Aunt Ellen's seashore world. Mr. Easton, a scrawny Yankee with a cloth cap and a ropy neck, drove us up in a station taxi that smelled of livery stable. He never spoke. The high point of the drive, the point that one sat on the edge of the seat for, came as we rounded the long curve in the road from Harborport and saw before us, below us, like a cup of blue water, like a great blue stone set in the pink granite cliffs, Cod Harbor. "Oooh," we squealed in unison, year after year, for this, too, was a rite. From there it was only a short way to the weather-beaten gray steps that led up to The Barnacles.

Aunt Ellen, a tall, spare, New England lady with hair caught up on top of her head, as though while running at full speed in a gale, would be standing at the top of the steps to meet us, arms outstretched and her soft, wrinkled face sweet with welcome; and, just behind her, Bessie. Bessie was Irish, but Bessie was different from other maids; she was created entirely to give me, personally, pleasure in life. After she had wrung my mother's hand and mine, wrung the corner of her apron, smiled all over her beet-red, shiny face, said of me, "Sure, she's grown a foot," she would disappear abruptly into the dark regions behind the dining room; I knew why, and hugged myself. I was here.

My Aunt Ellen's greatest care, during our visits, was to give my mother the rest she so needed. She always engaged an extra servant for our visit — a fat cook down from Boston — so that my mother need do nothing, nothing. *Rest, darling Rosa, rest; put your feet up; lean back; don't make an effort; can't I bring you something — a palm-leaf fan, an afghan?*

Meanwhile I would be playing on the floor with the blocks, the Aunt Ellen blocks. They had belonged to three generations of children and were unlike ordinary blocks, being plain, smooth, natural wood, shaped like bricks, with one, out of the fifty or so, cut out into a curve on one side so that it could be used for the top of a bridge, for a pinnacle. Presently Bessie would appear, as I had known she would, bearing a large pitcher of tinkling lemonade and a plate of her paper-thin fairy gingerbread. This was even more like it. I set to, while the ladies sipped a little from their glasses, and Bessie declared, "Ah, Miss Rosa, it's terrible how Miss Ellen will go. She's been running like the wild deer." For my Aunt Ellen, also, did too much. All grown-up ladies of my acquaintance did too much. I listened calmly, since that was the way the world was, meanwhile reaching for a fourth cookie and holding out my glass to Bessie, who cried, "Ah, the little darlin'!" as if I had done something remarkable. I smiled, and went on munching.

Aunt Ellen's house was large and airy and stark white inside. The bedroom floors were covered from wall to wall with straw matting; the bedroom walls were plain white plaster; and after I had gone to bed — we carried candles up to bed in that house — and before my mother had come up to join me, I would lie in this cool, airy bubble of a room with the windows thrown open to the seashore night, to the breathing of the sea in and out against the shore, and the faraway clang of the bell buoy off Cod Point.

In the morning Aunt Ellen waked us with a knock at our white-painted door. "The Order of the Bath," she would call. "Rosa, will you go first, or Nancy?" When it was my turn to go in the bathroom, I would climb up on the white wooden chair and look out of the small, high-up window at the morning sea. At that hour, about half past seven, the lobster fishermen would be rowing home out of the mist, from their pots, in dories — standing up, rowing frontward, with a stiff, jerky motion. The window, so high in the wall, was like the window in a horse's stall, I thought. It was extremely agreeable to imagine that one was a horse looking out of the window at the ocean. It seemed to combine everything vigorous.

Breakfast was eaten off blue-and-white china in a flood of sunshine from the eastern windows. My Aunt Ellen had visited at one time in Charleston, South Carolina, and had adopted such of its customs as fitted with hers; thus we had hominy with our finnan haddie for breakfast. Here was another rite: the instant Bessie had passed the hominy, one whisked a lump of butter into it, buried the butter until it was melted, and then ate the buttery, bland cereal with the salt fish. I drank milk; my mother and Aunt Ellen drank Indian tea. Muffins were passed, yellow and steaming hot inside, and strawberry and gooseberry jams from S. S. Pierce's.

I rose from the breakfast table girded for the fray. My Aunt Ellen's voice spoke the dulcet, the awaited, words: "Rosa, I thought it might be nice if Nancy had a new pail and shovel for the beach; hers from last year seemed rather rusty." For some reason that I have never plumbed, it was thought suitable that I should be given a new pail and shovel every summer, and this in a New England world whose truest motto was "Wear it out; use it up; make it do." I would then walk down the road to Cod Harbor village with my Aunt Ellen, to Trigg's Store, where pails and shovels were to be had. We walked hand in hand, my stringy old aunt and I, along the road between the fish houses on the seaside, where the fishermen sat mending their nets, and the moors on the upper side, redolent of wild roses and bayberry and sweet fern. This was the morning of the world. " 'Morning, Miss Hale," the old men in their oilskins would reply to my aunt's bow. "How is your rheumatism, Mr. Danforth?" she would inquire. "Nothin' extry, nothin' extry," the old fellow answered. We swung our hands and occasionally essayed skipping, for Aunt Ellen was of an indomitable breed and one, moreover, that did not concern itself with appearances. That a New England spinster, whom I, at any rate, considered elderly, should arrive flushed at Trigg's Store with her pince-nez askew and her hair even more sketchily suspended than ever was quite in order to her; Miss Hale had seen fit to skip. We stood, hands still enclasped, in front of the old-fashioned, paned show window; inside were fish nets, floats for fish nets like huge glass bubbles, reels of green fishing line, American flags to wave on Independence Day (Aunt Ellen had her own huge one, which we always hung from the upstairs porch on the morning of the Glorious Fourth), Rock of Gibraltar candy, rock candy on a string, toy lobster pots, spools of sewing cotton, and, splendidly centered in the window, a pail and shovel, classic, immutable, patterned with agreeable running children or clowns, red-lined. Possessed of them, I swaggered home.

Later in the morning came the moment of going to the beach. My mother, who had, of course, been resting, took me. Her dress was white linen, cut princesse over the hips, long and full-skirted. She wore a mushroom-shaped hat with a chiffon veil to protect her skin from the burning seaside sun, and carried a red cotton parasol, which was kept, at The Barnacles, in the coat closet under the stairs, along with the umbrellas and a gold-handled cane. Arrived at the beach, she disposed herself upon a whitened, polished granite boulder at the top of the slope of sand, adjusted her parasol, leaned back upon her hand, and looked pensively out to sea where, Aunt Ellen always said, there was nothing between us and Spain.

I myself then proceeded down the beach like an infant juggernaut, slow, deliberate, and relentless. I must have worn a variety of dresses during those years — I can recall striped ginghams and blue cotton crepes — but those pink rompers are what I chiefly remember, which shows you how far back it all goes. Pail and shovel firmly in hand, day after day I would approach the prospect of sand, sea, and sky: a vast spectacle, of which I felt easily the equal if not the superior. Words cannot express my pleased confidence, which verged on the bullying. The nearest is, the world, this world, was my oyster, or perhaps clam. That was what it was to be a child on the beach at Cod Harbor.

Hours passed. I built sand castles surrounded with

moats through which the tide sent surging currents, aqueducts that carried the water from one round dug-out pond to another. There were probably other children, at least sometimes, but of them I have no memory. It was I vis-à-vis the beach. I made sand cakes, round, golden, and studded with pebble plums; these sand cakes looked so delicious that I once bent and took a bite out of one, so entranced was I by my own creation. It was a real shock to find not warm savory plum cake in my mouth but all that grit. Perhaps it was at such rare moments of disillusion as this that I would glance up the beach toward that lone, slight figure on the rock — pensive, feminine, swathed in chiffon. I was always aware of her there, my lovely mother, so appreciative of the bits of ocean-worn green and purple glass I brought to her; so tender, so exhausted.

After lunch, which I greeted, once I could be pried away from the beach, with the lusty appetite of a buccaneer, we went to our room for rests. Aunt Ellen was firm about them. She was wonderful with children and invalids; she knew just what they needed. I was supplied with picture books, with the family blocks, and with Aunt Ellen's button box, to stay me as I flopped energetically about my narrow bed with its white seersucker bedspread. My mother lay supine. Occasionally she would draw a long sigh, and I would stop what I was doing, with the beginnings of terror. Those heart-rending sighs! But she never complained. At three o'clock we would rise, and sometimes we would be rowed by Aunt Ellen about the harbor in a skiff painted pale blue with a white inside, like the airy colors of a bubble. My mother reclined against cushions in the stern, her hand trailing in the cold water, her skirts held up with the other hand from the bilge in the bottom that swished fore and aft as Aunt Ellen rowed with a steady creak and a squeak of the oarlocks. I was planted in the bow, facing front, like a figurehead; my spirits, quite recovered, ranged rakishly over the crests of the little blue waves in the direction of Spain, which I could not actually see but took on faith, and where it would be nice to row to one day.

Or we would go blueberrying. The blueberries grew on low bushes up on the moors above The Barnacles, interspersed with wild-rose bushes, bayberry bushes, and sweet fern, dry and pungent. We picked into tin pails, and mine was, of course, my glorious beach one, shovel and all, since it was wrong to part them; however, I seldom got more than half a cupful. There was too much to look at. When you stood up from picking, you could see, over the tops of the wild-cherry trees, the sea, calm, flat, and blue; the big elm tree that grew by the turn in the road to the harbor; the chimneys of The Barnacles. One did not need a compass not to get lost up here. Then there were the cows Mr. Danforth kept up on the moors. (It was their milk I drank at meals.) They grazed beyond the stone wall that marked the boundary between Aunt Ellen's land and Mr. Danforth's.

One warm, still, peaceful afternoon I found myself, on rising from a clump of blueberries, face to face with a large light-tan cow, who stared at me as she chewed steadily with a rotary motion. My surprise was less than my curiosity; I advanced on the cow with interest and a confidence bordering on the truculent. But at that moment my mother saw us. "Nancy!" she called. "Darling! Mother's right here. Run!" I glanced over my shoulder at her, on the other side of the stone wall, and back at my new acquaintance, perplexed. "Run quick!" the sweet voice cried. "I'll help you over the wall." So I ran. I clambered over the rough granite stones, harsh with lichen, with my mother's gentle arms assisting my fat legs. The pale-brown cow continued to rotate her cud and to gaze after me reflectively.

We ate the blueberries that night for our supper, with sugar and cream, by the light of four candles — in Canton china candlesticks — that had round blue-and-white shades. In front of me the dining-room dresser displayed its rows of china, all of it blue and white: Canton, Willow, Copenhagen, Delft, and the onion pattern. Outside in the dusk, the sea sighed as it breathed in and out against the beach. The foghorn from Harborport began all at once to low. And by the time we had finished supper we were fogbound; outside the windows the fog pressed and billowed like surges of cotton wool. Aunt Ellen rose and lighted a lamp. "Smell the fog," she said. And indeed the fog had a special smell of its own, like the ordinary salt air but stronger, redolent of seaweed, damp, and dead fish. I loved it. We were in a private world in our nice snug house. The fire twinkled upon the hearth, the lamp shone yellow and oily beside Aunt Ellen as she read to me from *Treasure Island,* and my mother lay, smiling faintly, upon the parlor sofa with her feet on a newspaper, resting. All too soon it was time to send me up to our chilly, airy, white bedroom with a candle in a brass candle saucer. The shadows flickered menacingly in the corners of the room, which was like Billy Bones's room at the inn, and when I went to brush my teeth, the fog pressed against the horse-stall window to get in. I finished my ablutions hastily and leaped into bed. I did not dare to blow out my candle, but left it flickering where it stood on the captain's table, occasionally flaring sharply, as if someone had entered the room. . . .

But I never heard my mother come upstairs, or open the window, or get into bed, so I could not have been very frightened. And in the morning the sun was always blazing as we followed the Order of the Bath and descended the stairs to the cheerful dining room. Once more I was my morning self, tough, hearty, and invulnerable, ready to meet all comers, ready to advance on the beach with my pail and shovel, taking on sea, sand, and sky on my own terms.

It was these memories that assailed me so violently as I came across the anomalous sight of a pail and shovel in an inland Southern shopwindow; only, as I have said, they seemed less like memories than like an upsurge of energy, bringing into my busy, humid Southern life the smell of salt, the sight of blue water. So you can imagine how extraordinary it seemed, how like the neat intermeshing of destiny, when I got the letter from the Perkins people asking if I would like to rent The Barnacles, which had once belonged to my late aunt. You can see how I can hardly be blamed for the irrational feeling that I was *meant* to take it. The pails and shovels had been like a building-up to that letter. The Perkins people said that they were primarily interested in selling, but wanted to give me an opportunity to rent for a season in hopes that I would buy the old house, with which they were sure I had many pleasant associations, etc., etc. My husband nearly expired when he heard what they wanted for rent; he doesn't realize what houses fetch along the New England coast. But I had heard the click of destiny. For the moment the conviction was stronger than I was; besides, all the arguments were so good — the children's health, we would have sent them away to camp if this hadn't come up, a vacation in a new place for my husband when he could get away, and, actually, me myself; because I *am* exhausted. I had to take The Barnacles. It only goes to show how childish one can be.

Because, of course, as I am sure you have already guessed, the whole thing has been a great flop, a disappointment, a disaster. If I'd been in my right mind, I would have realized that nothing is the same when you are grown-up as it seemed to you when you were a child — especially when, instead of being as free as air, you have a thousand things to get done and, obviously, haven't time to go staring at views or basking in the sun. I can just see any house I live in, with four children, if I relaxed my efforts to keep the place organized for one moment. Bedlam.

And so this summer has been, for me, instead of the dream of childhood delights I was foolish enough to imagine, an almost unmitigated ordeal. Nothing works in this old house, for one thing. I can't see how dear old Aunt Ellen ever put up with the plumbing; the man has had to come over from Harborport almost every week since we've been here. And dirt! When Aunt Ellen finally got around to having the house wired for electricity, she was silly enough to try to economize, with the result that we have hideous tubes containing the wires running all over the old walls and ceilings, catching dust; the walls are none too attractive at best; bare plaster shows every mark. If I were to buy this old wreck of a house — which heaven forbid — the first thing I would do would be to rip out all that straw matting on the bedroom floors; when I think what must be underneath it after all these years, I shudder. Like all old houses, this one hangs around one's neck like the Old Man of the Sea. Of course, Aunt Ellen had servants. But nowadays . . . I've been driven — "druv," as the old Yankees used to say — all summer. I've hardly had time to look out of the window, let alone go down and sit on the beach. We do go to the beach, of course — I *take* the time for a swim now and then, and then there are the wienie roasts the children give for their friends. But it doesn't look the same any more. I suppose it's because I'm grown-up.

There *was* that time I was sick in the night. It must have been something I ate — a clam from the steamed clams we'd had for dinner. I've tried to show the children a little of what the old New England customs are, but they don't really care; they have other interests. They're Southern children, for one thing. As we drove around the corner that opens up on Cod Harbor, the day we arrived, after that long exhausting trip, I couldn't resist giving the old "Oooh" at that lovely, cool, pale-blue sight; but naturally to the children it just seemed as if Mother was taken a little dotty. They like it all right here, of course; they're in with an active crowd at Harborport, tennis players, and there's square dancing at the town hall every Friday night. But I was talking about the night I must have eaten a bad clam.

I was sick as a dog in the night — a foggy night it was — and it felt eerie and sad being up alone in this old house at two o'clock in the morning, with the fog-horn groaning across the moors from Harborport and the fog pressing white against the little high-up window in the bathroom. It was almost as if everybody but me was dead, and I was all alone in the world: sad, a little frightening, and queerly peaceful. I felt like weeping when I went back to bed.

Next morning I was weak. "Alma," I said to my four-teen-year-old, "you'll have to bring me something on a tray." She looked scared — they always do, as if the world was coming to an end if Mother isn't up and doing. She brought me a tray of coffee and some toast. I was on my feet by that time, but shaky, and I carried it out on the side lawn and set it down on the granite slab that used to serve as a table long ago when Bessie would bring us tea out there in the long, shady, peaceful after-noons.

Well, it was lovely. Over the tops of the beach-plum bushes I could see the ocean lying calm in the morning sun, swinging to and fro forever. There was a sort of hum in the air that I remembered, a hum made up of the sounds of bees and of hummingbirds and the hum that the sun makes shining. Otherwise the morning was very still. I don't know where the children had gone. I could smell the sweet fern up on the moors; the scent came drifting down on the salty breeze. I still felt weak and rather ill; but peaceful, happy. I leaned my head back in the deck chair where I was sitting and rested. It was such a beautiful morning, almost worth eating the bad clam for. I could have stayed resting in that chair all summer, while the white gulls wheeled over my head and slid down the air currents toward the sea.

But you have to keep going. Even though it was a big mistake to take this white elephant of a house, the only thing is to make the best of a bad job. There's not much more to the summer, and when it's over, I can tell you, I'll have learned to appreciate my nice, modern, efficient house, all on one floor, in Virginia. You learn by experience, and in the meantime we must just grin and bear it.

I think the hardest part is the way nobody co-operates with you. Of course, you can't expect it of children, and it doesn't matter so much when you can do most things for yourself, as I can at home, but up here there isn't, among other things, any washing machine, so I've had to try to find somebody to do our enormous family wash this summer — not only sheets and so on, but shirts and starched dresses and filthy dungarees of the boys. I suppose the children expect me to do it, but I'm not made of iron; I'm really not. The women I've found around here do it once and then never again, thank you; not a wash that size. Today I thought I'd found somebody, a Portuguese woman that the butcher told me about over the telephone. She didn't have a telephone herself, so I got the wash bundled into the back seat of the car, and the children pacified for having to wait for the car to go to Harborport, and drove down to Cod Harbor and found the street number the butcher'd given me — and then, of course, there was nobody home. I was outdone.

I just stood there in the road, wondering what to do

now. I didn't exactly see my surroundings, there was too much on my mind, but I could sense them around me — the white houses, so bare and stark; the bleached trunks of the gnarled locust trees, like whitened bones; the cold, blue, mournful sea that lay beyond and below the village of Cod Harbor. I began to walk a few steps down the road, past a house or two, looking idly around me. Everything looks so bleak, beside the sea; the atmosphere is colder, whiter.

One of the houses had a shop in its ground floor, and I stared abstractedly in at the things in the dreary, untidy little show window — fishing lines and such — while I tried to decide what to do with the wash. I was frustrated by everything. I was tired out. You'd think I would have got the whole idea of Cod Harbor out of my system for good. I almost hated it.

But when I saw that pail and shovel in the shop-window, when they burst upon my consciousness, my heart stopped beating for a queer joy, in spite of all I have been through. There they stood, *the* pail and shovel, tin, with figures dancing round the red-lined pail, and the shovel painted bright shiny red: enigmatic, irrelevant, inscrutable, ineluctably thrilling. They seemed almost to quiver with a mysterious significance, and as I stared at them the old, boundless, roistering mood of power responded in me — tough, rakish, and as impervious as a tightly sealed clam.

3

I WORRY ABOUT IT STILL, EVEN TODAY, THIRTY-ODD years later. I close my eyes to go to sleep at night, sometimes, and I am back at the old, disintegrated sand pile where I lost it, digging in the dirt-mixed sand with my fingernails to find my little ring.

It was tiny, a little girl's ring that was said to have belonged to the Empress of Austria. I suppose that would have been Elisabeth, the beautiful one who climbed mountains. It was given to me, I think on my eighth birthday, by a family friend whom I called Aunt and who was herself so erect, so blond, so high-voiced that I thought of her privately as a princess. I was told that she had bought the ring in an auction room in Vienna and brought it home — all for me.

The ring was gold, with a curly banner across the top which was set with five little turquoises. The gold setting of the stones was etched or engraved; it gave a delicate and lacy effect. I thought it was the most beautiful ring, the most royal ring.

"Far too good for a child to wear," my nurse said firmly. I can see her entwining her fat red fingers as she said it. "You won't be wearing it out to play, that's one thing."

But the thing was that I did. I was compelled to after her saying that. For nobody — certainly not she — could understand the love I had for that ring, and the absolute impossibility of my ever losing anything so precious. I wore it when I went out to play in the shed that adjoined the old barn and connected it with the abandoned milkhouse that was now called my playhouse.

Getting a playhouse, even a makeshift one, had been a sort of victory a little while back. Our only neighbors, the Wilkinsons, had a daughter named Mimi, who had a real playhouse, one built for the purpose: a tiny model of a cottage, with little green shutters at the windows, a shingled roof, a door with a shiny brass knocker engraved MIMI, and, inside, miniature chairs and a table upon which Mimi, a girl with natural ringlets, set out tea parties with real Dresden china made for children's use, china with pink rosebuds which were unendurably thrilling — pink rosebuds and gold rims.

Ours was not the place for that kind of thing at all. We had nothing that was modern, nothing that was fascinating like rosebuds on little new china teacups. Our big white house seemed to settle down deeper into the ground with every spring freshet. The barn was red. The place had once been a working farm, but all that was left of that now was the stanchions in the lower barn; the horse stalls in the upper barn, where one could stand and look out of the little horse windows over the swamp at the melancholy woods beyond; the market garden of rhubarb that came up doggedly year after year, no matter how many boxes of furnace ashes were dumped upon it (the rhubarb ended by coming up out of the ground at least six feet higher than the original garden had been); and the little house at the end of the woodshed, which had once been used to prepare the milk for marketing. There was a sort of slot at the front of this milkhouse, and the cans had been shoved out through it into a big box with a lid, where they could be picked up by the men who took them away. But of this I had only been told. Now there was no activity on our place. The pines in front of the house sighed and whistled in winter, the dandelions came up like little suns all over the lawns in springtime, the swamp turned from gold to crimson to purple as the summer passed sadly by, and in autumn the pumpkins lay rotting on the ground down below the lower barn.

I had to have a playhouse. I wept. And so the abandoned milkhouse was swept out, some of my nursery furniture was moved into it, and an ornate Victorian knocker was screwed on to the weathered board door that would not quite close, and it was officially referred to as my playhouse.

What was it that was wrong? It was not really a playhouse, to begin with — but I had imagined far wilder excursions than this required. I made the effort; I imagined that the too high shelves inside, where cans had been stacked, were really shelves for my own needs, to put books and toys and tea-party china on. I imagined that the bulkhead which contained the slot for pushing out the cans was really a window seat.

My mother gave me some china to use for my own efforts at tea parties. Rosebuds were what I yearned for, rosebuds were what I dreamed about at night. Small, neat rosebuds on a field of glistening milk-white china — *little* china, made for children. What I got was probably much nicer. It was the odds and ends of an old broken-up adult tea set — orange-and-white china with gold arabesques. I set it on the too high shelves — the plates on edge against the wall, the teacups in a row, the saucers in a pile, the teapot turned so that the broken spout did not show. It was probably very beautiful. But there was nothing, there could have been nothing, that would take the place of pink rosebuds.

Then I was given my little blue ring. It was a ring meant for a little girl to wear. It was real gold, and real turquoises. It was beautiful, and it had belonged to an empress.

It belonged to my hand. It was just the right size. In the morning sun, when I went out to play, its five turquoises shone in a curly row. Even all these years later, I can remember looking at it and feeling satisfied, complete, and happy.

It was probably not the first day I wore it that I lost it, but I did not have it very long. I went to play in the old sand pile that moldered away in the inner corner of the shed nearest to the barn. The sand pile was the remains of several cartloads of sand that had been dumped there, but since there was no frame to hold the sand (such as Mimi's sand pile had) it had sifted, filtered away, become mixed with the dirt of the woodshed, disintegrated, spread out; it was another of the things I had that had something the matter with them.

I don't know why I went to play in the sand pile at all. I was too old, and this was my playhouse stage. But sometimes I did go and play in it, in the scattered remains of my babyhood, just as sometimes I went and slid into the hole under the foundations of the barn that I had discovered when I was four — not to hide any more, not for any game, just to be in there and feel it around me again.

I went to the sand pile again, at the wrong age, and, whether the first time or a later one, I lost my little ring playing in it. The loss did not strike me all at once.

I came in to lunch, and my nurse said, "There. Will you look? You've lost your beautiful gold ring with the stones in it, just as I told you you would."

31

I said nothing. I looked at my horribly bare hand and looked back at her, not showing anything. I didn't want her to see anything. Because I was convinced that it was because she had told me that I would lose my precious possession if I wore it out to play that I had lost it. I didn't want her to know this.

"I know *exactly* where it is," I said. "It's not lost at all."

And in a way I did know exactly where it was. It was in the sand pile somewhere, and the sand pile was not more than ten feet wide, even in its disintegrated condition. It had to be there. I looked and looked — that day and other days, too — with a hollow, painful feeling inside me because I had lost my precious possession. At some point, I must have given up.

But I never completely gave up, because years later, in my teens, I would suddenly remember my ring, the one I had lost, and would go out to the sand pile, by now almost obliterated but still a definite area to me, and dig and dig. It had to be there. I never found it, but it was there just the same, somewhere in the mingled sand and dirt, within a definite space about ten feet square.

Once, I dreamed that I had found it. It was when I was a young girl going to dances, and the dream was about the most irrelevant to my life that could be imagined. But when I woke, with the clear memory of finding the ring and seeing it lie in my palm with its banner

of five little blue stones, my excitement and the verisimil-
itude were so great that I went out to the woodshed —
in a beige crepe-de-Chine dress, I remember, that reached
my knees; high heels; and my hair shingled — and began to dig once again. Then the telephone rang for
me, or someone drove up in a car. But after the dream
it was not finding it that seemed unbelievable.

Even now, in another part of the country, I sometimes remember my ring and wonder why I could never
find it. Today, for example, I took a walk in this Southern springtime, filled with the sound of the persistent
mourning dove and the occasional thrill of the wood
thrush. I passed the brook, which is called a run, and
the thicket of bamboos that grows beside it, and mounted
the gentle rise that leads on past the Lambeths' house.
The Lambeths have a lovely house — old, built of pink
brick, but all made fresh, all charming and inviting; inside, their floors gleam, their chintzes are trimly fitted
to the chairs, and they drink their whiskey out of silver
tumblers with gadroon edges. I would love tumblers
like that, but they must cost a fortune. As I rounded the
curve just before the entrance to the Lambeths' house,
I thought I would stop and pay them a call. It would
be fun to sit before their crackling fire and drink their
whiskey from one of those enchanting tumblers, and
perhaps come to know them better. But as I came abreast
of the drive, I saw that two cars were parked near the

door. The Lambeths already had callers. I felt a little hollow, and passed on.

When I made the circuit that brought me home, I felt thirsty and got myself a drink of water. My glasses are a sorry collection, the odds and ends of a number of broken sets. I went upstairs then and into my room, where I tidied up a little before lying down to take a nap. I don't know why it is that Mrs. Hildreth, who makes my slipcovers, can never make the arms fit properly; the cording lies unevenly upon the frame of the chair and gives a sloppy appearance.

I lay down, and as soon as I closed my eyes, there I was again, years and years later, back in the old woodshed of the place where I grew up, scratching and clawing at the sand pile, trying to find my little blue ring. I'm sure there is not as much sand, nearly, left there any more as I see when I close my eyes. There may not be any sand at all; the place is sold, and the new owners may have fixed everything up, torn down the shed, perhaps even put up a new, properly fenced-in sand pile somewhere for their growing children. I don't know.

Perhaps if the old sand pile *is* still there, one of the new owner's children will one day really find my ring, for it is there somewhere. Perhaps the child — a little girl — will be poking about with a tin shovel and will turn up that scrap of gold with its five little blue stones. I wonder what she will make of it.

4

WHEN I WAKE UP IN THE MORNING IN THIS VIRGINIA town, the children are all calling good-by to their fathers going off to work. I can hear the cars being started up — there is an old Buick next door that takes its time and makes a deep-throated, portentous coughing — and the chorus of dozens of children up and down the block calling, in their infant Southern accents, "Ba — Ba — Ba," like a flock of tiny, excited sheep.

One spicy, promising morning last September, one of the little sheep was not calling "Ba" when I awoke but, instead, a sort of chant of triumph; I lay still to hear what the words were. The child was shouting, "I'm going to school! I'm going to school! I'm — going — to — *school!*" — each reiteration growing shriller and more incredulously ecstatic. I jumped out of bed and went to the window to see. The little girl was just climbing into the car beside her father. Her brand-new tin lunch box got in the way of her knees; she was wearing a new blue coat and a blue hat to match. I think she must have been seven. As they drove off, she poked her head out of the window and proclaimed once more, like a lark rising, "I'm going to school!"

I got back in bed, thinking, I wonder how long that will last. I wondered what it is that happens, so soon, to take the bloom off that rapturous approach to education. It doesn't take long — a matter of weeks, sometimes — before the permanent slump comes, the dismay, the reluctance, the dread that I have propelled my children through during the remainder of their school careers. Of course, some children don't seem to mind, I thought, but I doubted whether they were the ones who would carol so joyfully on the first day of school.

I tried to remember what had happened to me after my own first, blissful entrance. I can remember that first day, how round the suns of the autumn dandelions shone on our front lawn; I myself was four. And yet it cannot have been much more than two years later when I used to pull on my long brown cotton stockings for school, lace up my brown leather boots, feeling such nausea that I would have to stop and lean my head against the frame of my old maple-sugar-colored bed. What happened in between?

I remember certain preliminaries to my first day of school — old Mrs. Stanford saying (when I told her as she passed our house "I'm going to school!"), "At your age? Oh, I'm sure you're going to play school." I answered indignantly, "I'm *not* going to school to play.

I'm going to school to *study*," showing I was not under any misapprehensions. And when someone else (who?) asked me, in an indulgent voice, what I was going to learn at school, I replied, "I'm going to learn sweeping and French."

And I was taken to tea beforehand with the head-mistress, an English lady who had settled in New England and opened this school for boys and girls up to about fourteen. She was very British, and so, I realize now, was her school. My mother and I had tea with her in her study while, I suppose, I was looked over. The study was dim and crowded with papers and books, and made still darker by an adjoining conservatory filled with plants and vines, vivid green in the late-afternoon sun. Of the plate of cakes that had been brought in on the tea tray, there remained one cake, round, pink-frosted, glossy; my fingers stole toward it, but Miss Cavendish's voice halted me then, for the first time. She said, "Nancy! The last cake is for Miss Manners." I stared at Miss Cavendish, not entirely taken in by this anthropomorphic projection of hers. She was a big, stout woman, somewhere in middle age, with gray curly hair, who wore a black cloth shirtwaist and skirt and, over them, academic robes.

But even this warning of discipline to come did not faintly dim my bliss and pride and self-importance the day I first went off to school — on foot, in those days, holding my father's hand.

It was the only school I knew, so I took it for granted, but, looking back at it, many things strike me as extraordinary; for example, the daily assembly in the gymnasium, all shiny, varnished yellow oak, when Miss Cavendish, in her scholar's robes, read the Order for Daily Morning Prayer out of the prayer book to us little Unitarians and Congregationalists, only partly leavened by a sprinkling of Episcopalians, and when, occasionally, we small descendants of Revolutionary patriots stood up and sang "God Save the King." We sang lots of songs not, I am sure, generally sung in American schools, when we were sitting on the cold, slippery golden-oak bench that ran around three sides of the gymnasium — "John Peel" and "The British Grenadiers" and a number of instructive jingles that were supposed to teach us history the easy way. Of these, I can remember all of only one:

> Little Jimmy Watt
> Saw the cover of a pot
> Jumping up and down like a dandy.
> So he went and learned a trade,
> Built the first steam engine made,
> And the whole world found it very handy.

Furthermore, when Christmastime came around, the ruling spirit of the holidays was referred to as Father Christmas, and I remember sitting in the darkened gymnasium in a folding chair beside my mother, watching the older children put on the Christmas play. It

38

concerned Saint George and the dragon, and included characters named Holly and Mistletoe, and could probably, I now realize, have been classed as a pantomime. A year or two later, I myself, dressed in pink cheesecloth, with a gold tinsel girdle, represented Discretion in a school rendering of *Everyman*.

But none of these curious phenomena had anything to do with rubbing the bloom off my glory at going to school to study. I viewed them as one views the whole unaccountable spectacle of the world at four — with phlegmatic calm. They made as much sense as anything else. Only the black-robed figure of Miss Cavendish, reading prayers in her British voice in the chilly yellow gymnasium, became daily more frightening, less human.

We, the youngest children in the school, had as our classroom a large room on the south side of the ground floor. The school had been a private mansion in which a few changes had been made. We sat on little, chunky, green-painted chairs around long, narrow tables to do our reading lesson or to sing:

> All things bright and beautiful
> All creatures great and small
> All things wise and wonderful
> The Lord God made them all.

In the middle of the morning, we went into an adjoining pantry, where we were served either cold milk or hot cocoa. The cocoa was served in tall, narrow, white china mugs with a blue pattern; I remember how the scum on top of the cocoa clung to the bowl of the spoon as one lifted it carefully off, for I had learned, listening to the others squealing or groaning, that scum is disgusting. With the drinks went Huntley & Palmers biscuits called Petits Beurres. The winter sun streaked through the southern windows to the right; the window at the left was partly blocked by the end of Miss Cavendish's conservatory.

To this dark corner, we pull our green chairs in a circle to take our French lesson from Mlle. de Mostuéjouls, who comes to the room for the purpose; other classes are going on in the rest of the room behind us. We learn phrases and sing French songs:

> Savez-vous planter les choux
> A la mode, à la mode?

I am sitting beside a little boy named Charlie Mellon. I stare at him, transfixed, for he is the most beautiful person I have ever seen — black hair, blue eyes, pink cheeks, long, sweeping eyelashes. Prompted by my delighted admiration, I lean over and kiss him on his pink cheek. Mlle. de Mostuéjouls sees me.

At once, a torrent of horrified French bursts forth, and I am snatched from my little green chair and made to sit at the farther end of the circle from Charlie. By Mademoiselle's expression — shoulders raised, nose wrinkled

— and the squeals and groans of the boys and girls once she has communicated her opinion to them, I learn that I have done something as disgusting as scum on the top of cocoa is. I sit quietly at the far end of the circle of children, over where Miss Cavendish's conservatory leaves me in the shadow.

The next bad thing I remember happening was the lie I told about the cat.

I am sitting at one of the long tables, I think in a reading class. Suddenly I have a fearful urge, a need, to assert myself, and I remark that at home I have a cat who can read and write.

"Oh, Nancy!" says the teacher. "No cat can read or write. Don't tell lies."

But it has become true. I *have* got, privately, at home, a remarkable cat who actually can read and write. In my mind's eye I can see her, the book propped up before her wise and whiskered face.

"I'm not telling a lie," I say. "She really can read and write."

The trouble that came to me after that! I was called, alone, into Miss Cavendish's study, where she sat, a thoroughly terrifying object by now, at her desk, in her robes.

"Nancy, you are telling a lie."

"No, I have a cat who can read and write." I clung to it as if everything — stability itself — depended on it.

My mother was got in touch with, paid a long call shut away with Miss Cavendish in her study, and emerged with red eyes.

"Nancy, you mean you can *imagine* a cat who could read and write," my mother said.

"No, I really have —" But here something broke. It was because I was looking at my mother. Watching her handsome, distressed face, I know that in the place where she and I live, there is no cat who can read and write. It is very much of a shock to realize this.

So then there are apologies exacted, to Miss Cavendish, to the room teacher — "I'm sorry I told a lie." And after that there is a distinct difference, not only in the way I feel about school but in the way school feels about me, for I am branded as a liar, unreliable, at least for a time.

Standing up with the others in a long line in our classroom, on a day when no sun comes through the windows to the south — perhaps it is snowing — I am given a word to spell, and I spell it wrong. The girl next to me spells it right, and I exclaim spontaneously, "Oh, I knew that!"

"Don't lie, Nancy," the teacher says. "If you'd known it, you would have spelled it right."

But I *had* known it; only forgotten. It was an injustice. The next class was in singing, and I remember how the hymn we sang so often seemed now overlaid with slime, so that I felt a sort of disgust toward it.

"All things bright and beautiful — aagh . . ." it sang itself in my head.

In that first year, we small children saw really very
little of Miss Cavendish except in assembly. The following year was different. The following year, to get
to my classroom I had to climb one of the pair of curv-
ing, formal staircases that mounted symmetrically from
either side of the big hall to the upper rooms. Now
Miss Cavendish herself taught us English, and we took
arithmetic instead of "numbers," and in addition to
learning French orally we had to read and write a little;
we had the regular penmanship teacher now, who also
taught sewing to the girls, and we took a course from
Ambrose, the school handyman, in something called
sloyd, which meant an infant version of carpentry.

Also, we were faced with the existence of the Brigade. The Brigade was a very small group of the best
children in school; that is, to belong to it you had to
get high marks and, in addition, you had to display
characteristics like honor, trustworthiness, responsibility for the younger ones. Those who had attained membership were given pins to wear — pale-blue enamel
pins in the shape of a triangular banner, with wavy
undulations, which bore the motto FAIS CE QUE TU
DOIS. The year that I mounted the grand staircases for
the first time, all the members of the Brigade happened
to be boys. No girls had been considered worthy.

43

I longed — we all did — to be chosen for the Brigade, but with those blots upon my record I never expected that I should be. And I was not, until late in that year, perhaps in May.

I was standing at the top of one of the staircases, preparing to descend for recess, when Miss Cavendish bore down on me like a black-sailed ship. I don't know why she didn't call me to her study, but she didn't.

"Nancy," she said, in her clipped British accent, "I hope you will make a great effort to live up to the honor which is about to be conferred on you. You're to be a member of the Brigade, my child." She put the precious pin into the palm of my limp hand, and retained my hand in hers. She was speaking quite loud, as usual, and several of my schoolmates gathered. "It's not to be taken lightly, you know. As the only girl"— she said "gel"—"you will appreciate your position. And now," she said, turning my hand over in hers, "go into the bathroom and wash those dirty fingernails and hands."

The humiliation — meted out at such a time, in such circumstances — felt for the moment greater than the honor. I walked down the long second-story corridor to the big, old-fashioned, unconverted bathroom and, with my face crimson and burning, turned the water on in the basin. I laid the badge of the Brigade on the glass shelf, which was above my head, and dipped my hands in the water. Slantwise through the glass I could read the motto on the pin — FAIS CE QUE TU DOIS —"Do what

44

you ought to." I was longing to be at home. It was the first time I remember getting that familiar longing. I no longer wanted to be at school. I wanted to go home.

Nowadays, of course, schools are better, or at least less eccentric, than the one I first went to. But, one way or another, the same sort of disillusion befalls those who perhaps too joyfully set off for their first day of school. This February morning when I woke up, in addition to the chorus of bleating baby lambs I heard a voice raised in wails and screams of protest —"I don't want to go to school! I *won't* go to school! I hate school!" Poor, wretched child, of course those pitiful assertions of the will did her no more good than they have any other child who roars out what he will or won't do. I looked out of the window and saw my little September friend being dumped into the front seat of the car by her father, still dressed in that brave blue coat and hat, clutching automatically at the once proud lunch box. Off they went. I figured that it had taken her about five months.

Naturally, one has to go to school, and one does get something out of it. Of my own three aims, as declared at the time of starting, two seem to have been accomplished — I did study, at school, and I did learn French rather thoroughly during a total of twelve years of it. But I never learned to sweep, alas, and I can't yet.

45

5

To no one, however partial and prejudiced, can Boston ever have seemed more utterly the hub of the universe than it did to me when I was a child in our house twelve miles out in the country and my father would come home from his studio and do what our family expression called "tell his times and tell them long." Boston seemed not only central to cosmogony, it appeared to my infant mind — beguiled by my father's indubitable and antic faculty for telling a story — dazzling with lights, coruscating with wit, and giddy with gaiety. Any realization that the somewhat bleak and drab city I saw when I was taken soberly to the dentist in no way resembled this glittering metropolis never arose to trouble my englamoured imagination. My father's Boston was a Boston of clubs and banquets, of artists and great hostesses, of hansom cabs and famous wits, and I continued to believe in it, dizzily, for years.

With it for a background, my own life in the country seemed an impoverished and paltry routine. I walked a mile to and from school every day, past the jail in which during most of my childhood Sacco and Vanzetti were confined. If the weather was bad, I was taken in a livery-stable hack that smelled of hay, driven by old Mr. Harvey, who had a long white beard. I skated, drearily, round and round Weed's Pond in the freezing, glassy afternoons while a crimson sun hung low above the horizon, casting a lurid and fateful-seeming radiance over the impassive snow. I was given my supper and later my bath by Miss Lovejoy, an English lady who lived with us in return for the care of me. Miss Lovejoy had a strong British character and demanded white pepper at meals, declaring the black to be unfit to eat. When she came to us, the first World War was still going on, and she had a map of Europe in her bedroom, in which were stuck small flags — pins — marking the battle lines, which I was not allowed to touch. On afternoons when I did not skate, Miss Lovejoy took me for long, long walks about the countryside, miles and miles, past a turkey farm, and a place where there was an idiot girl who smiled frighteningly, and a gate with the sign BEWARE OF THE DOG. After my supper, when Miss Lovejoy gave me my bath, she would, if she was in good humor, sing to me, always the same song:

Into pretty London came an Irishman one day;
As the streets were paved with gold, so everyone was gay.

This solecism bothered me terribly, even in the earliest days, when I played with my celluloid swan and green ducks in the old, footed bathtub. But if I objected, Miss Lovejoy would only start to cry, "Come along, come along, don't be slouchy," which meant the end of my nice, warm bath.

It was generally after I had been put, flat, clean, and still moist, into bed that my father would arrive home from his day at the studio. My bed was narrow, with four posts of a wood that looked exactly like maple sugar; I licked it once, but the likeness did not extend to taste. At the immense sound of the front door being opened and banged shut, the stamping off of snow in the front hall, the loud and genial shouts of arrival, I would shoot upright in my bed like a jack-in-the-box. "Papa!" I would call, and in a few minutes his heavy, reassuring tread would come up the stairs, into my room, and around the corner of the wall to where I could see him, large, heavy, with a walrus mustache. After embraces, my father would sit down beside my bed to tell me stories. These fell, very loosely, into three categories, of which I was only faintly aware: the true stories, the legendary stories, and the stories that he simply made up as he went along because he was bored with the reality. I could generally tell, when his eyes held a glazed look and he began to hesitate and say "Aaaaah" between sentences, that he had taken off and was careering among the stars.

48

My father's position vis-à-vis Boston society was a little different from that of the usual Boston gentleman; although born into the large family of a famous Unitarian divine, he had, instead of going to Harvard like his brothers, gone to Paris to study art at Julian's and the Beaux-Arts. This step was so unusual as to have been suspect even to his father, in most things a liberal; my father was not supplied with funds for this doubtful enterprise, but supported himself in Paris to a large extent by copying. He lived in the Rue des Saints-Pères with a group of other young Americans; the ascent into the garret where they slept was by way of a ladder nailed against the wall, up which the young men would climb, a lighted lamp in one hand and a pitcher of water in the other. When my father told it, the ascent was so terribly difficult that it sounded nigh onto impossible; but he always insisted they accomplished it. On his return to Boston, flushed with the wine of art and with that sense of confident aspiration which the artist Gainsborough expressed on his deathbed —"We are all going to Heaven, and Van Dyck is of the company"— he married my mother and took a large corner studio in the Fenway Studios. They produced me and moved the family's living arrangements to the country in consideration of the benefits of fresh air to the young; but my father continued to go daily to town to paint in his studio or to teach at the school of the Boston Museum of Fine Arts, and saw, in the social way, during those ten or twelve years of my childhood, a mixture of old friends from Paris student days, old Boston friends from even earlier, a number of the great Boston hostesses, and a proportion of rag, tag, and bobtail that only my father could have dredged up — borrowers of five dollars, unattractive models with ailing mothers, bumptious painters without talent, and types of the pure species bore, who fastened upon my father with an unfailing instinct for recognizing the kind heart and the dread of wounding. Not least in the canon of Boston stories were those of sheer, typically Bostonian stupidity, which somehow made the enchanted vision I held no less enchanted. At the Tavern Club a very Boston Mr. S——— was told the riddle of "Why is a penny like John the Baptist?" the answer to which was "Because it's one cent by God." Mr. S——— was utterly convulsed by this joke and made off instantly for the Somerset Club — he had really been out of water at the Tavern Club — where he repeated his delightful new story, but with a fatal difference; for he inquired of his audience, "Why is a nickel like John the Baptist?" and when they looked expectant, answered himself, "Because it's five cents, God damn it."

The Tavern Club was mostly a place of congregation for writers and newspapermen. The St. Botolph Club was a meeting place for many of the Boston artists. The Somerset Club, to which my father did not belong but often went, was of a different stamp. At one stag dinner, he often said, repeating the story with slight modulations, changes, so that it was almost like a new story every time, he had disgraced himself before the chief steward, or headwaiter, of the Somerset Club. Orders were being taken for dessert. *Meringue glacée* was ordered here, *coupe aux marrons* there. When the dining-room chief came to my father, he inquired, "And you, sir?" My father was devoted to strawberry ice cream, which he thought of by another name. "I will have some pink ice cream," he replied. The headwaiter bellowed across the dining room to the underwaiter, in tones of terrible contempt, "This gentleman will have some *pink* ice cream." In some versions of the story the entire assemblage turned and stared, with frigid astonishment; in others they only laughed. But always, more than what the Somerset Club steward thought of my father, the story rather conveyed what my father thought of the Somerset Club.

He was fond of repeating the motto of the Tavern Club as a model of neat phrase: "Fill your empty glass; empty your full glass; I cannot bear to see your glass either empty or full." But on the whole he preferred the St. Botolph Club, which in an irreverent mood he would call the St. Bottles. It was said that on one occasion an Englishman visiting Boston had been put up at the St. Botolph Club and, going into its lounge one day about five, had ordered tea. The steward looked nonplussed, but rallied quickly. "Yes, sir," he said.

There was a long, long pause. The pause became *so* long that after an hour the Englishman felt justified in inquiring where in blazes his tea was. It transpired that time had been required, first, to send out to Pierce's for the tea and, second, to study, in a recipe book, the rule for making it.

That world of clubs! To me at home, hugging my knees in my four-posted bed, it wore an aura cosmopolitan, male, and rakish, altogether irresistible and delightful. My father could not have been called by his worst enemy an athlete, so that aspect of club life played little part in the stories. All I remember ever hearing of the athletic side was a silly song, which at the time I hearkened to with grave attention:

> Dick Hodgdon's not much at athletics;
> He can't even play cowboy pool;
> And they say at the old Union Boat Club
> That he's usually beat, as a rule.

The Boston painters of the day were my father's principal companions in club life — Tarbell, Benson, Paxton. How dashing, how major, those now nearly forgotten names sounded to me! Occasionally a European figure in the world of art would make an appearance in Boston. I remember my father bringing home to spend the night William Rothenstein, later knighted. I did not see him until the next morning. As I was eating my porridge at the round dining-room table, he entered

with my father; he looked like a Chinese, with slant-
ing eyes. "Oh, I love little girls!" he cried, and thrust
his head directly in front of my face with an extreme,
Oriental smile. I screamed.

Another visitor to Boston from foreign shores figured
in a story about the world of the great Boston hostesses.
This hostess had managed to secure a real plum, a visiting celebrity whom my father always called, in the story,
Count Pallavicini, though I doubt that that was his
name. In his honor the lady engaged to play at her party
the Boston organist Malcolm Lang, both because of
Lang's distinction and to show off her magnificent instrument. About this stage in the story my father's eyes
would become glassy. "The night of the party arrived,"
he would continue, "and — aaaaah —" Lang performed,
the applause was enthusiastic, but the lady wanted Count
Pallavicini's personal expression of appreciation and,
hurrying up to him, cried, "Oh, Count, wasn't Mr.
Lang's playing superb?" The aristocratic visiting Italian
replied, "Yes, yes, he was well enough-a. But to play-a
ze organ," he went on, waxing ardent, "and manage-a
ze monk', all ze sama time, *zere* was ze genius."

At this juncture I would be leaning forward upon
one nightgowned elbow, in my four-posted bed, tense.
With a child's unerring instinct for the human as above
the anecdotal, I would more than likely ask, "And what
did *she* say?" My father, the point of his story thus
ruined, would pull down the corners of his mustache

53

and chew them in exasperation. It grieved me to annoy him, but I did so long to know what happened next.

But the stories I loved best were not really stories — in the sense of anecdotes — at all, but the recounting of the glorious, magic, Lucullan evenings my father and mother spent when they dined in town. Here my fancy really soared, undamped by cynicism, untickled by humor, straight into the pure wild empyrean. If my parents had had any idea what agonizing pleasure they used to give me when they came to bid me good night on their way out to an evening in town — my father in tails and a boiled shirt, my mother as beautiful as a seraph in pink satin embroidered with passementerie, her pink satin shoes pointed at the tip and with deeply curved French heels, her scarf spangled gauze, her wrap changeable velvet with ostrich feathers round the neck — they would surely out of mercy have dined out continually. In actual fact, they went out rather seldom.

My father's best friend was an architect, of an old Boston family, who had studied at the Beaux-Arts in Paris. He and his beautiful golden-haired Irish wife, who had been an artists' model and whom I called Aunt, were fond of dining at the Boston restaurants, with my parents, in a day when restaurant dining was not frowned upon but unusual, Bohemian. My pretend uncle was a great gourmet, a connoisseur of wines. I remember particularly that to preface their little dinners he favored *vermouth mélangé.* So I was told; and since no one explained to me what *vermouth mélangé* might be, I thought of it as pale green with foam on top; nectar, in short.

In the days before there was a me, they used to dine at the old Thorndike, famous for its game. But the Thorndike burned, I think, and by the time I began the years of swallowing tales of Boston night life in great draughts, it was the Touraine that they chiefly patronized. Afterward, perhaps, they would go to a musical comedy — the two gay friends from old Paris days with their beautiful wives, one fair, one dark. This pleasant custom they carried on for years. My father had the faculty for remembering the score of all the musical shows they saw, and while he was taking his cold bath in the morning, he would render songs from performances running far back before my birth, until the house rocked:

> Then meet me on the beach at Narragansett . . .
> Country girls, city girls,
> Dull girls, witty girls,
> All sorts of pretty girls, coming down to dive.
> When you see the little beauts
> Sitting in their bathing suits
> You'll be glad that you're alive . . .

Or, more swooningly:

> Oh, won't you come and play wiz me
> And stay wiz me
> Make hay wiz me?
> I've such a pretty way wiz me . . .

I do not think the phrase "make hay with me" really appeared in the proper version of this song, however. I think my father made it up, to rhyme. When he could not remember the words of a song and could not think of anything to rhyme either, he filled in with the phrase "my boys":

> I wonder who's kissing her now.
> I wonder who's teaching her how.
> I wonder who's gazing into my boys,
> Yes, my boys, yes, my joys!

so that he could complete his rendition of the songs that they used to hear in Boston theaters and music halls in those nights of the early century when they would dine out.

The mere mention of meals being taken of course made my infant pulse quicken. I would squirm with a vicarious greed in my bed and interrupt the story by asking, "And what did you have to eat?"

My father did not like being interrupted. He would shut his mouth and pull down one corner of it. Sometimes, in retaliation, he would then tease me by intoning, "Well, first we had sooooop, and then we had fiiiiish, and then we had meeeeeat . . ." But sometimes he would relent and tell me about the marvels that they had to eat and drink at those little dinners — the game ducks, cooked purple rare; the Château d'Yquem, the Piper Heidsieck, the *pâté de foie gras,* the Baked Alaska, the Danziger Goldwasser, the, ah, the nightingales' tongues.

Actually, in this phase of the legend, it was my own imagination that created the atmosphere of that glittering, brilliant, worldly Boston that never was on land or sea. After they had gone out to dinner — trailing chiffon and the smell of bay rum — and I was left in my dark room to try to go to sleep, my mind would travel into the world I fancied they had entered. Down Commonwealth Avenue they swept, its double boulevard bordered with winking white lights, its great brownstone houses blazing with illumination, front doors being opened and shut continually by tall butlers. Past the Public Garden they proceeded, and down Boylston Street, to the restaurant of their choice, palms in the forecourt and flunkies on either hand. "Table for four!" was the cry; and, casually, with glances cast backward and the intimate exchange of bons mots, they would find their seats, be bowed to by the major-domo; the two ladies would lay long white kid gloves carelessly upon the damask tablecloth. An orchestra played, behind potted plants; acquaintances — rich, handsome, distinguished — nodded recognition; the first course was produced, on silver platters with domelike covers. The words for all these things had been told me, in the stories; but the colors, the glitter, the atmosphere, at once rich and sparkling, I supplied myself.

Lying there in my dark room, I would try not to remember the story about Mr. H——. Mr. H—— was one of my father's dead-beat friends, the sort of painter who was always saying he would "knock 'em dead" with a new picture, and never succeeded in selling anything. He lived off lessons and, perhaps, off touching my father; I always thought of him as having a ragged, drooping mustache. At one of those little dinners at the Touraine, my father had seen H—— across the room and, in leaving, stopped to speak. H—— was dining off rare roast beef and claret. "Have to treat myself to something decent once in a while," he said, jovially. "Keeps my spirits up, you know. Mrs. H—— cooks up a batch of macaroni every Monday morning and it lasts us the rest of the week. She and the little girl can stand it but, by Gad, I can't. *Ça m'ennuie,*" he added, with a ghastly attempt at old Paris bonhomie.

I would switch my mind sharply away from this picture, for it was gloomy, and of all things I feared gloom, such as I felt in the air on those occasional nights when my father's heavy footsteps, coming upstairs, instead of turning into my room, went along the hall to my mother's, and I could hear the low, urgent murmur of voices in there. Once I got up and stole along the hall and listened to my father telling my mother of the discouragements he encountered in the always forbidding field of trying to be an artist in Boston. Since then, there was always the frightful doubt in the outer fringes of my mind about whether he was happy after all, or successful, or sought-after.

The really awful, the unbearable part of the Mr. H—— story was that a few months after the encounter in the Touraine Mr. H——'s little girl died — of eating macaroni, presumably. It made an unpleasant stain upon the cloth of gold of one's vision of Boston night life.

When I grew up and began going to parties in Boston myself, it was quite another world that I encountered: a sedate world, painstakingly simple, lined with patronesses, policed by chaperones, decorous, unostentatious, and pleasant. But juxtaposed ideas sometimes do not conflict at all; it was some time before it occurred to me that the parties I attended bore little or no relation to that land of glitter and glory I had imagined my parents going off to when I lay as a child in my narrow fourposter.

I had, of course, entered the real Boston, or *a* real Boston. My days were passed in going to morning practice sessions for the chorus of the Vincent Show in the downstairs ballroom of the Somerset Hotel; attending debutante luncheons at which it was fashionable to rise before dessert and leave, taking the centerpiece flowers with one; tea dancing to the strains of "That Certain Feeling" with Harvard seniors at Shepard's Colonial; going to dances in the evening given at one of the hotels or at the Women's Republican Club, or, perhaps, out at the Brookline Country Club, among surroundings that meant merely health and fresh air to us. We wanted to be world-worn and decayed, and so we escaped to go slumming, wearing our most blasé expressions, at the American House in Scollay Square or, our nerve up, down at the Argonauts Club on Rowe's Wharf. We got to bed about three and slept late, waking to see that snow had fallen in the night.

When at last it emerged into my consciousness that this life, though busy, was not at all the Boston of wit, gaiety, and sparkle that my father's stories had, with my collaboration, created, the realization was accompanied by a feeling of bewilderment and of resentment. For I was left with a whole airy metropolis on my hands, shimmering, inappropriate, iridescent, fitting nothing, as if I held a fabulous ruby necklace that had been declared bogus. What could you do with it? Where could you put it?

6

I FIRST CAME TO VIRGINIA AS A VERY YOUNG ENGAGED girl, a regrettable number of years ago, in order to see my fiancé receive his doctor's degree at the university. We drove down from Washington in the old Stutz I owned in those days — arklike, with an H shift and a right-hand drive — by way of Culpeper, over a dirt road that was then the northern approach to Charlottesville. In Orange we stopped to spend the night with the family of one of our prospective ushers, in a beautiful old brick country house with a romantic name. My imagination, already stimulated by the view of the Blue Ridge, the great thousand-acre fields, the red clay and the snake fences of the South, was utterly beguiled by Lucasta.

Our bags were taken in by a fat, shiny, black, white-haired butler called Pinky, who beamed and offered my fiancé a drink; we were received by the most delightful of hostesses, who called me "dear child"; into my room as I dressed there drifted, through the open window, the mingled scents of boxwood and honeysuckle. Supper was served by the light of a dozen candles, guttering in the light June breeze as we ate tobacco-colored ham, fried chicken, spoon bread, yams; and for dessert Pinky, in his white coat, passed us ice cream made from fresh strawberries and solid cream, in a huge old ornate silver bowl. It all came close to Paradise.

After dinner we were offered drinks. I refused; at home, girls of my age were not allowed to drink anything except an occasional cocktail, and champagne. "Oh, come on, honey," my fiancé said. "A little drinkin' whiskey and branch water never did anybody any harm." But I really did not want a drink, and said so.

Then the moment that had to come came. My hostess, smiling charmingly to show it didn't matter, remarked, "Don't press her," and, to me, "I can see you're a real Yankee."

My first impulse was to look behind me to see whom she was speaking to; my second, to ask, "Who, me?" Actually, I did neither; but it had simply never occurred to me that I could be called a Yankee.

I was quite a big girl before I ever even saw a real Yankee. My parents' friends were Bostonians who commuted to town; the tradesmen in the village were, for the most part, Irish; our maid was Swedish, our gardener was Italian, the farmer up the road, Mr. McLeod, who was so stern with his three daughters and said if they didn't get home by ten o'clock at night they need never come home at all, was Scotch. The other farmers were Irish — Mr. Sullivan, Mr. Mulcahey — except for the fearsome Mr. Lee, who often reeled home past our house with tousled hair and bloodied nose, and he came from New York State. Some of the ladies I saw on Sundays after I was old enough to stay through church were real Yankees, I was told, and the man who came to chop our wood, Worthy Barlow, was often referred to in my hearing as a typical Yankee; he walked all the way to and from work, nearly ten miles, to save carfare, and sometimes as he whacked away at the wood on the old chopping block we would hear him muttering, "If the logs had heads, I'd chop 'em off."

But although I had seen so few of them, I had heard many stories about real old Yankees. Basically, "Yankees" meant countrypeople who were of English settler stock. Their most salient feature seemed to be that they were characters. Their habitat was in particular New Hampshire and Vermont, although they were scattered over the rest of New England. Their pronunciation of the English language had a peculiar salty flavor, as illustrated in one of the earliest stories I was told. My Uncle Robbie, as a boy of six, had been taken along to call on one of my grandfather's parishioners, a real old Yankee woman. She was sick in bed, and my grandmother made her some tea while they talked. As my grandmother was about to hand her a cup, the old woman said, "I mostly drink it from the sarcer." My Uncle Robbie, a notably tenderhearted child, thinking to put her at her ease, felt it necessary to remark, "We say sarcer, too."

Most real old Yankees were farmers or seafarers by the time I was born, but in my grandfather's family, back in the days when some Yankees still went into domestic service, there had been a manservant named Fullum, many of whose tart-tongued phrases were quoted to me as I grew up. I have seen a photograph of Fullum, in his frock coat, with a sparse beard that made him look like Uncle Sam. During the terrible potato famine in Ireland, when boatloads of immigrants arrived weekly in the port of Boston, my grandmother was reading the newspaper at breakfast one morning, and the news made her exclaim, "Oh! How dreadful! A whole shipful of those poor people has been drowned!" Fullum, who was looking over her shoulder at the headlines in his customary familiar way, as he passed the muffins commented, "It don't matter. They was Irish."

Most of the best stories of the real old Yankees, in our family, came from the South County of Rhode Island, where my grandfather used to own a summer house and where my father and his brothers had gone for the summer as boys. My grandmother was by way of being an invalid, and the household was often presided over by my Great-Aunt Susan.

There was Mr. Perkins, whose chestnut horse and

two-wheeled cart used so often to appear opportunely on the long, white, dusty South County roads; lifts would then be offered to the little footsore boys, and they would go rumbling through the flat, beautiful, singing countryside, drinking in the wisdom that emanated from Mr. Perkins. He was given to making philosophical aphorisms, punctuated by admonitions to his horse: "There's two kindsa strong. Strong like Samson, and strong like a skunk. Git up, there, what ye 'baout?" The little boys adored this Yankee character so passionately and quoted him so reverently and incessantly at meals — "Mr. Perkins says this" and "Mr. Perkins says that" — that my grandfather had to make a rule: No boy can mention Mr. Perkins more than once during dinner.

But my Aunt Susan's special friend and admirer was Mr. Browning, he of the long prophetic beard, the Yankee ingenuity at fixing anything at all, of the unforgettable twang — "Braownin'" we pronounced his name in our family years after the old man was dead. "Waal, Miss Suse," he remarked to my aunt on one occasion, "got to gwup t'Providence, testify in some gret legal dewings."

"Oh, Mr. Browning!" Aunt Susan exclaimed in dismay. "And I was counting on you to fix the shutters. Just say yes to everything they ask you and hurry back quick."

"Nope," he replied, "I ain't a-going to agree to nothin'."

Another time, when Aunt Susan asked Mr. Browning to do some job he would really rather not have done, he replied with a brand of gallantry wholly Yankee, "Waal, Miss Suse, you air a lady, and shall be treated as sech."

My Aunt Susan enjoyed eating her meals out-of-doors, in a day when not many people had acquired that habit. One fall, she stayed on in the South County, and was sitting alone over a late breakfast when she heard the rumble of cart wheels going by down in the road, and up through the sharp, winy air of early autumn floated Mr. Browning's voice, loudly addressing a deaf companion: "Nope, she ain't crazy. She likes her victuals that way."

My first real encounters with the Yankees occurred at my Aunt Ellen's on the North Shore, where we went in the summer to visit her by the sea.

There had been a time when that part of the New England coast was inhabited solely by Yankees, but now the great majority of the people near where we lived were Finns, descendants of a large migration brought over in the second half of the last century to work the granite quarries. The old Yankee names survived in the families of the lobster fishermen; not many of the Finns went professionally to sea. One of the first items on my agenda, as a child arriving at the seashore each year, was a visit to the fishhouse down on the rocks where Mr. Asaph Bentley and Mr. Washburn and Mr.

Starr sat mending their lobster pots while the salt breeze twitched at their long white beards. They were dressed in oilskins and rubber hip boots. "How do," they would gravely remark as I approached, my hands behind my back, my pigtails switching from side to side; and then we would all lapse into a long comfortable silence, a Yankee silence, broken only by the occasional ejection of a stream of somebody's tobacco juice. Once Mr. Washburn, who was the oldest and had the longest beard, showed me, in June, an iceberg, out on the horizon, through the spyglass that he kept handy.

All these gentlemen went out at daybreak every day in their dories, and when I got up in the morning and looked out of the seaward window, I would see them coming home through the mists that clung low over the pale-blue ocean, standing up in their boats and rowing frontward, with stiff, jerky jabs of the oars. Although they went out in all weathers, none of them could swim. If queried about it, they would explain that 'twarn't no sort of use; with them hip boots on, they'd drownd anyhow.

Mr. Asaph Bentley lived up behind us on Bentley hill, in an old house that had solid wooden sliding shutters, originally installed to deflect Indian arrows. In a rafter of the attic was lodged a cannon ball shot from a British frigate standing out in the cove in the War of 1812, presumably only to announce its arrival, for Mr. Bentley's ancestress of those days had seen the British

67

tars come ashore shortly afterward and start rounding up the cows she pastured out on the point. They showed signs of being about to take the animals on board ship. Incensed, Mrs. Bentley had stamped out on the point and demanded to see their commander in person. The sailors obligingly brought him ashore in a gig, whereupon Mrs. Bentley explained to him that she could by no means afford to lose the source of her children's milk and of part of her income. The British commander quite saw the cogency of her arguments, and bade his men desist at once. They all rowed off, leaving Mrs. Bentley happy and satisfied, so their intentions could not have been very warlike.

But Mr. Asaph Bentley, who was a widower, did not care much for historical recollections like this; he liked to drink. He and his son, young Asaph, who worked "in to the granite company," sat up every night over a bottle and an oil lamp. Old Asaph got up early to go lobstering; young Asaph rose later, and before leaving for town always took the scraps from their last night's huggermugger bachelor meal out to the hens, in whatever dish the food happened to be in. This went on for years, until young Asaph, at the age of about forty, married. He was considered to have married beneath him — a Portugee. But the girl had her good qualities. For one thing, she cleaned out that pigpen of a house. It was generally thought that the first layer of dirt must have required a shovel. She also began retrieving the dishes that for so many years had been taken out to the hens and never brought in again. "She digs 'em up," old Asaph reported to my Aunt Ellen, "and makes 'em into sets." In a short while, the Bentley ancestral china had been reassembled: old white ironstone, Lowestoft, Staffordshire — things dating from the eighteenth century.

Although among the people I grew up with it was considered a great compliment to be compared to a Yankee, to be told one was as shrewd or as thrifty or as honest as a real old Yankee, not all the real old Yankees I knew were admirable characters. There was Jim Huggins, down the road, who married Maud Lovett and made her life a hell. She had been seen, by her neighbors, running out on the point in the middle of winter with her hair streaming and Jim Huggins after her, yelling he would kill her. Jim Huggins was not even thrifty. He owned four extra dories and left them lying bottom side up on the rocks by the cove with stones on top of them to hold them down in a gale, until they all rotted and fell apart, an action tantamount to blasphemy of the Holy Ghost in those parts. But even before the final disintegration of the dories Jim Huggins had taken off for the bright lights of Salem with a woman, leaving Maud Lovett deserted.

Maud Lovett belonged to the oldest family thereabouts — people whose land had been held originally by Indian grant, people who numbered among their forebears preachers, doctors, lawyers, and who had sent up members to the legislature in Boston. But no more. The Lovett family had fallen upon evil days, particularly since they had taken to marrying one another. Maud's mother and father, first cousins, had not spoken to each other — although they occupied the same dreary, dark-green house all through those lonely, frozen winters — for twenty years. Maud's sister Ella went up to St. Johnsbury and got a job working behind the counter in the ten-cent store but was dismissed for talking wildly, whatever that may have meant. Its meaning became clearer after poor Maud Lovett's desertion by her cruel husband, for she, too, began to talk very wildly indeed. She had moved back into her old home with her silent parents, but all day long she hung around the small house by the shore where she had been so unhappy with Jim Huggins. It seemed as if she could not bear to leave the scene of her undoing. She would pop out of the overgrown beach-plum bushes as I passed along the road on my way to go swimming. "Seems I have to stay araound here all the time," she would hiss at me. "Soon's I go, *they* come, with guns. Tried going in my own house t'day, but they've got it locked, *and they watch everything I do."*

It was frightening. It was a great relief to leave her behind, standing alone in the road gazing out at the blank blue sea, and to wave instead to Mrs. Washburn, who was also of ancient family but whose brains were perfectly good. Mrs. Washburn made delicious-smelling bread, and ginger cookies with which she was not too thrifty when little girls passed by. She was what my Aunt Ellen called a real Yankee lady; she knew about paying calls, in white gloves, and she was extremely proud of being, herself, a Starr. A Starr had once been governor of the colony. Mrs. Washburn's voice and accent were the true Yankee article: dry, flat, with a nasal twang; and she was brief-spoken. When she broke her leg and was confined to bed, my Aunt Ellen went to see her. "Bumped m'knee," said Mrs. Washburn.

These memories, and more like them, are the reason why, after living happily for so many years in Virginia, I still tend to jump when addressed as a Yankee, although of course I have long since realized that to everybody except New Englanders "Yankee" is a generic term including me. That my reaction is not without parallel in reverse was made clear to me recently when I read a story by Frances Gray Patton, a North Carolina lady, who told how it made her feel to be called a "cracker" by an uninformed Yankee. It made her feel, she said, stung.

When I am called a Yankee I don't feel stung; I feel disoriented. My head swims. I lose my sense of identity. I get the feeling that instead of being my usual conforming, conventional self, I am someone far more interesting, who speaks a pungent, if peculiar, English, who is slightly dotty, and who is a great character. I only wish I were.

7

I WAS LOOKING THROUGH A COOK BOOK IN SEARCH OF A dessert that would be quick and sweet — in a hurry as usual, because when those great boys come tramping into the house for their supper, they want lots of it, right away, and the dessert had better be a sweet one. Bavarian Cream, I read — but that takes time, stirring over hot water, and so forth. Baked Meringue Custard — not sweet enough. And then my eye fell on the next recipe, Charlotte Russe. I felt a little tremor of joy in my heart at the name, and in spite of the hour, I began reading through the recipe: ". . . combine eggs, salt, and sugar. . . . Cook until mixture coats spoon . . . cool quickly and flavor with vanilla. Fold in the cream which has been stiffly beaten. . . . The mixture should not be stiff enough to mold." Suddenly I felt furious at this heresy to the Charlotte Russe of my childhood, and I let the book shut over my thumb and sat thinking about the way it was.

Nobody knows, nobody can know, how I used to feel about the party dessert that appeared when my father and mother reluctantly, at long intervals during the winter, gave a dinner party. Not stiff enough to mold indeed! It was molded in a form with peaks and turrets, so that when it was turned out and stood, an object of beauty, coated with the ladyfingers that had lined the mold, it was like a turreted white castle, like a palace of sparkling dream as I walked round and round it where it was set on the dining-room table to get it out of the hot kitchen. In those days, no icebox could have contained anything so towering, so round, so fragile as the Charlotte Russe.

The table had been enlarged with leaves to make a long oval, and laid with special silver and glass for the approaching rite. For this was the way I thought of those decorous dinner parties, which I never witnessed but only heard from above and clothed in my mind with the veils of perfection. Places were laid for twelve. Instead of the plain glass water tumblers we used every day, at each place was set a high goblet of glass cut in a design of flower garlands, and beside it two wineglasses, one for claret, one for Moselle. The huge damask dinner napkins were folded in the bishop's miter shape and set in the center of the place plates — vast, chilly white, ruby-rimmed. The row of forks extended far to the left of each place. And in the center of all a great epergne of ruby and clear glass was piled with oranges, pomegranates, lady apples, and what my mother used to call deathbed grapes, big and black. On either long side of the centerpiece stood large cut-glass bonbon dishes with covers, on high stems; these held pink and white peppermints from S. S. Pierce's, and, lest the effect be spoiled, I was not allowed to have any until the day after the party. But I did not care; I would rather look than eat. I was allowed, earlier, to help lift the delicate sugary disks from the waxed-paper layers in the white box that had Pierce's gold shield on the cover and lay them gently in the bonbon dishes. There always seemed to be just enough.

On a side table were set out the plates for dessert — white, with a gadroon edge, and a single pink rose painted on each; the rose was now concealed by the thin glass finger bowl, set on a lace doily, flanked by a silver dessert fork and spoon. The finger bowls would not be filled — meaning a bare half inch of water — until just before dinner was served, and then a leaf of lemon verbena would be floated in each, to crush between the fingers at the close of the meal. Also at the close of the meal would be brought out the decanter set — an ebony box inlaid with mother-of-pearl — now decorating the center of the sideboard. When the front and top of the box were turned back on hinges, they disclosed a fairyland of myriad tiny gold-rimmed glasses on stems, set in a gilt framework holding, at the four corners, gold-banded liqueur decanters containing brandy, cherry brandy, apricot brandy, and crème de menthe. The guests would need such marvels, I thought, to sustain them after the high point of the dinner had been passed: the miracle, the ritual destruction of the Charlotte Russe.

Its spires and peaks were now snowy with whipped cream and sparkling with bits of red candied cherries and green angelica. Before the people came, it would be whisked away out into the unheated summer kitchen, where it was too cold to keep it for long. And then they would enter the dining room, I thought — the ladies in their evening gowns with low necks that showed a fascinating crack in front, the gentlemen in their tailcoats and glacial expanses of starched shirt. They would eat, with tablespoons, the cream of tomato soup with the dab of whipped cream floating on it, the oyster soufflé that my mother would have been praying about, the roast, served carved in the kitchen *à la russe,* with the tiny round balls of potato covered with butter and lemon and parsley, and then it would be time: therefore with angels and archangels they would topple the towers and eat the fragile and delicate substance of the Charlotte Russe. Sometimes there would be a few broken bits of it left the next day, but usually anything left over got consumed in the kitchen; except for once or twice, I never tasted the thing that looked more beautiful, more desirable to me than any food on earth.

All of this that I have described represented an enormous outlay of time and energy for my mother, who, if she must have a dinner party, wanted to have it nice. My father categorically resented all activities that took him away from the evenings he liked to spend reading; making dry-point etchings, under the unshaded glare of a blue bulb, with a diamond-point needle; copying the drawings of Watteau in red chalk. I found it almost incredible that they did not enjoy the prospect and the performance of these dinner parties, which so represented the great world to me, but as my father pulled on his evening trousers out in his dressing room he would call in to my mother while, in a camisole, she did her long, wavy, dark-brown hair before the oval mirror in her bedroom, "Well, it can't last more than six hours."

"Six hours!" she would cry, rising to the bait. "If they're asked at seven, it's bad form to stay after half past ten."

My father would wrestle with his boiled shirt as I stood in the open door of the dressing room; his stomach made the dress shirt buckle and bulge. He moved his shoulders uncomfortably under his tailcoat. "I believe in dressing for dinner every night, like the British in India," he said, "but not for a lot of tedious idiots. Well," he called in again to my mother, "a hundred years from now it will all be forgotten."

I would have had my supper earlier, off the kitchen table, while maids hurried and pushed past me, carrying silver that must be polished at the last minute, carrying colanders of dripping vegetables, carrying pots and pans to the soapstone sink from the stove, which was an old-fashioned black coal range with nickel trimming. Maids were always Irish in those days, and they were all named such names as Bridie and Lizzie and Nelly; I remember there was one named Norah whom my mother would get in for dinner parties because she could bone shad.

As I grew older, when the guests arrived I was allowed to come down and speak to them, dressed in my dancing-school black velveteen with the gold moire sash run through slots. I took the hand of each ravishing lady, each indulgent gentleman, in turn, kicking the floor behind me with one toe in lieu of a curtsy. The room smelled of the fresh roses the ladies wore tucked in their tulle fichus, and of the things the gentlemen put on their hair. They all looked, to me, excited and aware of the thrilling events before them — the unfolding of those napkins, the shattering of that Charlotte Russe; apotheosized, and not at all like the torpid people I knew as the parents of my school friends, reading the Sunday paper on a late-winter morning. Everyone looked stimulated, including my parents; but a little canker of sorrow told me that with them it was not sincere; they were not really thrilled, but bored, and wishing the dinner party were over. In those days, at least in our house, no one was given anything to drink before dinner, so I only stayed down for a few minutes. Bridie would come to the door: "Dinner is served, mum" — and there began the bustle and chattering confusion of going in to dinner.

I would climb the stairs to my own room. That was the last I saw of the dinner party; it was never the custom in our house, as I have read it is in some houses, for the child to come down for dessert.

When I was in bed, I would lie still, with the window open to the dark, snowy winter night, and let my feelings soar. I could faintly hear the hum of conversation in the dining room underneath me; when the door between the dining room and the kitchen was opened, a burst of laughter would float up the back stairs. The people at the dinner party were Olympian, seated around a Parnassian table loaded with the fare of gods. I could hear the footsteps of the maids, hurrying over the wooden floor of the kitchen to wait upon them. They drank from crystal goblets; their napkins were vast, satiny; their jokes were, surely, magnificent and immortal. And in the center of it all was, for me, the Charlotte Russe, borne into the dining room at the last by careful hands, inviolate, and then broken into with silver serving fork and spoon. I could see it happening — that perfection of whipped cream, cherries, and angelica, its towers fallen. Much as I loved the Charlotte Russe, I took pleasure in thinking of their shattering it. And when I in my turn became grown-up — enormous, invulnerable — I, too, would sit at dinner parties, be passed exquisite, trembling confections, break into them with fork and spoon without even looking, my head turned as I exchanged ineffable witticisms with the gentleman beside me.

78

I don't need to say that this flood of recollection that came on me as I sat in the kitchen with the cook book in my lap made me late with everything for the rest of the afternoon. The boys came in before I was half ready with their supper, and no dessert made. I can't imagine what led me to waste so much time, because actually there's nothing I want to do less than unpack all that china and glass that's been in this attic ever since the old house was broken up. And as for making a great, elaborate, extravagant dessert, I haven't the time or energy. I'm tired when I get the dishes done at night, and glad to follow my husband into the living room and read the evening paper. He's finished with it by that time, and the boys are upstairs doing their homework, and we can be quiet and peaceful in the family circle, hoping to goodness nobody drops in.

8

As I lie here, trying to get over this idiotic cold before the Hansons' party, my mind becomes restless and inattentive if I try to read; I set up a game of patience on a tray and even then it is as though my mind's eye were focused on some other scene; until sometimes I give up altogether trying to distract myself and simply lie here, resting, and letting my thoughts wander about as they will in my childhood, in the time when I was kept out of school so much by colds. I suppose there is a connection: I haven't had a cold in years, and I suppose this one reminds me, now, of those days when I had so many.

My mother was always very particular about taking me out of school at the first hint of a cough or a sniffle. So inconsiderate to spread a cold around, she used to say; but also my mother was a great one for prevention; she had some terrible inner picture of complications ensuing on the common cold: the house suddenly lighted up at night, temperature's gone to 104, run for the doctor, where's the croup kettle? I don't think I ever, during the period of which I speak, at least, had anything but the simplest sequence of sore throat, head cold, and the usual cough afterward.

I have no doubt but what I enjoyed staying at home, reading, and eating nice things, and not having to do anything. Any child jumps at the chance not to go to school; but my relief was a little deeper than that. This was the period when Geraldine Ames was riding high as a leader in our class, and she was the president of a club against me.

A child never knows quite why it is singled out as the one who is all wrong. There appear to be different reasons — in my case that my parents were painters instead of my father's being a stockbroker or banker, and that my dresses, which my mother made, had their waistlines up under my arms instead of around the hips — but the child knows inside that these are not enough. The real reason is cosmic: the child is *wrong*, that's all, the herd have named her so and there is nothing, there never, never will be anything, to do about it. I would come into the varnished-oak gymnasium for prayers at the beginning of school in the morning, and Geraldine, tall and pretty with long black braids, would catch the cloth of my dress as I passed her on my way to my place and give it a tweak and whisper "Crazy . . ." with that scornful and yet abysmally beautiful smile.

I remember walking down to school in the morning,

that winter, and coming to the patch in the road where it crossed the County Meadows, where the wind literally whistled across the flats and through the row of willows, and where, if the weather was zero, it was the coldest of all. It must have been January; I had on my brushed-wool cap-and-mittens set which I had been given for Christmas and which I had adored then and paraded before the mirror in, admiring its orange-and-green stripes, but which I took no further pleasure in since, one noon-time after school, as I was coming down the stairs from the classrooms to the cloakroom, I had found Geraldine and one of her devotees kicking my cap around. I stood rooted to the bottom stair, watching, my heart sick. "This yours?" Geraldine asked, picking it up and tossing it at me disdainfully. "Crazy kind of a cap." I wept when I got home that day, for the beauty that had gone out of my cap-and-mittens set, and for being in the wrong. When my father got home that night, my mother told him about it. "Buck up," he said to me. "You let them see that you're as good and better than they are. Stand up for good old you." But that was impossible; he did not understand. Geraldine was beautiful and in the right, and I was in the wrong.

That morning as I crossed the bitter windy County Meadows, school seemed to loom ahead of me like a heavy woe. The January gale went through my heather-mixture coat. Suddenly I felt a tickle in the roof of my mouth. I'm getting a cold, I thought. I hesitated for a moment, and then turned around to walk home again, obedient to my mother's dictum: "Always tell me at the first suggestion of a cold." I walked back up the icy street, up the hill to my warm snug home and my bed and the books that stood arrayed on my white-painted bookshelves. I don't think there is any question but that I was running away.

My mother believed in light, nourishing food for colds: poached eggs, warm and consoling on a bed of soggy toast; chicken broth; baked potatoes, like hot little stoves one could hold in both hands before opening them and spreading them with butter and sprinkling them with salt; milk toast — toasted white bread laid in a soup plate, salted, with hot milk poured over it; the butter from the toast rose and floated, yellow puddles, on the white surface; cream of wheat — and as I put the cream and sugar on I would remember the game my father used to play with me when I was tiny: Once upon a time there was an island; and then white rain came, and rained and rained until it covered the island almost all up; and then it snowed, and snowed and snowed. . . .

When I stopped sneezing, and my mother could persuade herself that I was not going to develop pneumonia this time, I would sometimes leave my bed, with its white-painted arms for putting books on, and go and lie on the chaise longue in her room.

Her room was papered with a white paper that had a trellis; at the top was a frieze of green ivy leaves. The bureau, one of the Victorian sort decorated with carved fruit, had been painted white, by my mother, and the grapes that formed the handles painted green, with brown stems; it was very beautiful. The chaise longue upon which I lay was covered in bright green satin, and had white woodwork, traced with a line of green. I had a brown comfortable, brought with me from my room, tucked around me, and wore my old brown wool dressing gown with a pattern of Indians on it: it was two Christmases old, and I had loved it once, but I doubted all my own possessions now; perhaps that was why I so particularly enjoyed lying on the green satin chaise longue in my mother's bedroom. I stared up at the ceiling, where some long cracks and a stain made a shepherdess with sheep and an old man with a long beard, like God. It was so beautifully clear and uncluttered up there on the ceiling, with no furniture; it was easy to imagine oneself walking about upside down, with free, skating motions.

Sometimes my mother would read to me. I remember Miss Edgeworth, Mrs. Ewing, and especially the historical novels of Charlotte M. Yonge. One afternoon she was reading to me from *The Chaplet of Pearls*, which was very exciting. The setting sun of midafternoon cast a red glow on the snowdrifts outside, which reflected back through the bedroom windows, pink all over the white trellised walls. That hour, of sunset in the middle of a snowy winter afternoon, always seemed majestic, frozen, almost final. . . . My mother was reading the part where Charles IX, from the staircase to his apartments in the Louvre, witnesses the murder of Admiral Coligny in the Massacre of St. Bartholomew. At least that is the way I remember it. It seemed terribly real to me; I could see the carnage, hear the shrieking in that frightful midnight. I stood on the staircase, I was the King, I stared down at the murder and the blood-stained Guises . . . only the staircase was the staircase at school and the murder was being committed in the cloakroom below.

After a while my mother stopped reading and I began to play with cards, on a wooden board intended for cutting out dresses; but it was not pleasant, the kings and queens looked nasty and ferretlike; I thought of the jeering stoats and weasels in the Wild Wood, in *The Wind in the Willows*. My mother came and laid her hand on my forehead. "You've got a temperature again," she said, and hustled me back to my own bed. I think I was feverish all that night. My father came and stood in the door to my room when he got home. "Poor old girl," he said. "Got a temperament." He never called it "temperature."

Sometimes, when I was getting well from one of those colds, I, too, used to draw pictures, only they were not very good. What seemed to turn out best was copying colored pictures out of art books of my mother's and father's; the color was what I liked to put in. I had two water-color paintboxes, one rather limited, left from my infancy, the other large and with handsome pans for mixing the colors. My father tried to encourage me to copy Ingres and Watteau in red chalk. But what I liked best to do was to copy the pictures of saints out of an old art calendar.

The reason for this was that I had been given some gold paint, and I particularly enjoyed painting the haloes round the saints' heads in thick, solid gold. I would sit at the upright black desk in my room, dressed in a great many sweaters for fear I would catch more cold, and prop the calendar, which was long and narrow, up against the pigeonholes, to copy from. First I made a drawing on my water-color pad of the saint in pencil, long and narrow and fitting into a pointed arch as in the picture I was copying; then I opened my paintboxes and began to fill in the colors, dipping my paintbrush in the jelly glass of water beside me. Most of the saints were men, with long gray or brown beards, blue or rich purple mantles, and white garments edged with the Greek key, which also gave me an opportunity to use gold paint. I always left the halo for last, and filled it in with the grainy, sparkly gold paint very carefully, so as not to smear, or run into the hair color. Sometimes, painting a halo and taking my time over it, I would wonder what haloes were, what they were supposed to be made of: whether they were hard and thin like gold plates, or just light radiating from the saint. They seemed to be a sort of label saints wore. I imagined that the label must represent the way saints were inside; they must have something inside that was round and shining and complete. One afternoon as I was painting a halo, with the electric light, which hung from the ceiling inside a Japanese lantern, turned on because it was snowing hard outside, I began to wonder how it would feel to have a halo on, round and gold and enveloping my whole head. But all I could think of was how a cold in the head felt — round, too, as a matter of fact, and enveloping; but thick and like cotton wool.

My mother came to the door of my room and said, "Bettina Nash is downstairs and wants to see you. I told her she could, I don't think you have any germs now, but be sure to sit beside the fire out of the draft —" I didn't wait to hear her finish. I was out of that room as fast as I could dash. I slowed down to enter the living room, though, of course. Bettina was dressed in thick sweaters instead of a coat; there was still snow on her shoulders and on the top of her red skating cap. "C'mon out, why don't you? It's good coasting this after," she said.

"I can't. I'm getting over a cold," I said, dismally, and she actually seemed to sympathize with me, for she said, "Gee, that's awful. Can't you get over it quick or something?" She went away, after a while, but something had changed, a chink had opened, for she was one of Geraldine's cohorts and she had come to see me. I can't remember even going back to that boring old saint, that afternoon or ever. I was never any real good at painting, anyway.

That afternoon a tide had turned, for me, for the next thing I remember is being one of Geraldine's cohorts myself. I don't know why she decided to accept me, but I remember basking in the precious peace of her approval, which we all sought avidly by agreeing with everything she said. "Dja see that new kid in fourth class?" she would say, as we stood about under the sighing pines in the schoolyard at recess. "She's *crazy*." "Crazy-looking thing," we would chime in; crazy meant anything wrong, anything different from the norm, which was, of course, Geraldine herself: pigtailed, gingham-dressed, belted at the hipline, scornful, *right*. I would chime in as loud as any of them, for now all was well, somebody else was crazy, not me.

These scenes, like the pictures from an old-fashioned magic lantern, are what have been running incessantly through the back of my mind as I lie here, trying to get over this stupid cold in time for Louise Hanson's party. It's too absurd; I *never* have colds. I suppose you could figure out that by having the cold I'm trying to escape from going to the party, since I know Louise hates me. I've been told the kind of malicious thing she says behind my back.

But I'm not a child any longer, to run away. My husband says, "What do you care? If she hates you, just give her the go-by." He doesn't understand. Louise Hanson gives the best parties in town, the most important parties, and I'm not going to let hurt feelings keep me from going to this one. Besides, if there's one thing all those memories prove, it's that you never can tell. For all I know now, by this time next year I may be Louise Hanson's most intimate friend — just the way I used to get asked to stay to supper at Geraldine Ames's, long, long ago.

I wish I could throw off this cold. It's boring to stay in bed, when you're grown-up; nobody brings you trays of good things to eat, not these days. I've read all the magazines, and I can't bear games of patience, really — those horrid little faces on the cards. There isn't anything to do, just lie here with my cold filling my whole head and feeling like some kind of cotton-wool halo. I suppose I could get up, cold and all; but then, it pays to be cautious. You never know what a cold may turn into.

9

I WRITE IN PRAISE OF S. S. PIERCE'S, THAT BULWARK OF a Bostonian's life. As these words speak themselves in my mind, the name Pierce is pronounced as though it were spelled "Perse" — S. S. Perse's — for that is the way everybody in my childhood world pronounced it, and the way my grandfather's parishioner Mr. Pierce pronounced it, and the way old Bostonians wherever they may be, in the Argentine or Alaska, pronounce it when they say to one another at breakfast, "We seem to be running out of tea. We must order some more from Pierce's." Today there is a tendency, even within the establishment itself, to pronounce it "Pierce" as spelled, and I once noticed an advertisement of theirs in which an arrow pierced something or other, as though to leave no doubt; the polite man who calls me up nowadays at my summer house on the North Shore early every Thursday morning to take the order that will be delivered by truck Saturday says, "Good morning. This is S. S. *Peerce*"; but to the true believer, the committed addict, the name is Perse.

In my childhood, when the firm appeared upon my consciousness, it assumed rather the aspect of the Royal Canadian Mounted Police in old movie serials; it was, or I felt it was, a lifesaver, a band of stanch and gallant heroes bringing nourishment to the stranded. This was because of the really remarkable record for regular deliveries that Pierce's had set for itself and lived up to. On the coldest winter Saturday nights, when the snow lay two feet deep all around our house twelve miles outside of Boston and was still falling, making of the one small street light a cross refracted through a haze of swirling snowflakes; when the local tradesmen had completely given up any attempt at deliveries since the day before, and I had got out my snowshoes from the summer kitchen with large ideas of rescuing the family from starvation come Monday morning (actually we had plenty of Pierce's cans on the pantry shelves); then — perhaps while we were eating our baked beans and brown bread at the round dining-room table — the back door would be flung vigorously open, steps would stamp into the kitchen from the entry, and bang! that reassuring crash of a big Pierce's delivery box, with slot handles, onto the kitchen table would be followed by the smaller bangs of its contents rapidly being taken out and set down. "Pierce's!" the man would call with a certain hearty, unvarying cheerfulness, and we would rise from the table, napkins in hand, and rush out into the kitchen to see him, snow all over his shoulders, face crimson,

taking the last things out of the box — the crock of strawberry jam, the wooden tub of butter — and preparing
to depart on his long, lonely route. "Do let me give you
something — a cup of coffee," my mother would cry, but
he always shook his head and laughed and said, "If I
stopped going, I'd freeze to death when I went out
again." Then the back door slammed, and the sound
of a horse's snort, the sound of runners would be heard;
for what always happened on those bitter days when the
local tradesmen failed us was that Pierce's, unable to get
its auto trucks through, either, hired sleighs from livery
stables and got through anyway with the delivery — a
standard that, for me at least, easily rivaled the dashing
boasts of the U. S. Mail.

But from even earlier, more indirect sources the legend of S. S. Pierce's had been impressed upon my infant
mind, when family stories were being told. Old Mr.
Pierce — Mr. *What* Pierce, I wonder — had been a pil-
lar of the South Congregational Church in Boston, of
which my grandfather was minister. (It was not really
Congregational at all, but Unitarian.) He and his daughter Miss Etta Pierce — always beautifully and suitably
dressed, it was invariably added in the stories — had both
been teetotal. From its founding, the grocery business of
which Mr. Pierce was head had dealt in wines and
spirits; but he entertained scruples about this, and finally
he came to his minister to ask whether it was, not wise,
not expedient, but right to sell liquor. This seems now

to me to have been an attitude, in the most prosperous days of Victorian materialism, comparable to that of his Quaker fellow tradesmen to the south. Incidentally, my grandfather's answer to him was that he should do so, since in any case people were going to buy liquor, and it was well that there should be one concern that could be counted on to sell nothing but the purest, the best. I suppose it is as a result of this decision that today a large section of the *Epicure,* the catalogue that Pierce's sends to its far-flung customers twice every year, should be devoted to the most excellent of French vintage wines and the most choice of spirits.

Another legend that entered the canon was one that I have never been in a position to verify — that for its salesmen, who have a reputation for considerate politeness to customers, Pierce's employs as often as possible small grocers who have failed in their own businesses. I like to think that it is true when I remember in how many gone-to-seed general stores, under the elms of how many dying New England towns, I have been treated with a particular brand of genial yet at the same time crisp and self-respecting courtesy.

My first actual encounters with Pierce's, the store itself, came when I began having to go in town, at the age of about nine, to have my teeth straightened. In those days the trip was an ordeal. First my mother and I took a trolley from the village as far as the Forest Hills Elevated Station. I never failed to feel carsick on the trolley, or to notice with a somewhat nauseated satisfaction the large, round, stone water tower we passed, which I thought of as the Bishop of Bingen's Mouse Tower on the Rhine; it was quite a shock to me when I grew up and drove a car to discover that there was on the other side of it no water of any description. At Forest Hills we ascended on the moving staircase to the bitter-cold, windy platform to wait for the next Elevated train; when it came, we took it as far as Northampton Street, where we got off and walked down into the street to wait on the corner for a streetcar to Copley Square, where the dentist's was. All this was necessary because the train schedule to Boston from the village where we lived was arranged to suit the convenience of business commuters, and carried no afternoon trains.

I am still haunted by that street corner where we waited. It was in a tough section of Roxbury. Saloons lined the street, with swinging doors; pieces of newspaper blew down the pavement in the freezing wind; and one day while we stood there a man came shuffling along *with no shoes,* with his feet wrapped in rags. I could not bear it, I could not take my eyes away; and after we had boarded the nice, warm, smelly streetcar, the memory of the man joined, in a special compartment in my mind, a small but growing company: the man with no legs, with leather-covered stumps, trying to sell pencils on a street corner, with a desperate expression that had convinced me that he never made a sale; and old Mr. Harvey, who drove the last forlorn livery hack in our town.

The aspect of the parts of Boston through which the streetcar passed changed gradually, from ghastly to sordid to merely dingy to smug, until at last we reached Copley Square and climbed the stairs to Dr. Bates's office. The rufous, foxy little dentist would give another turn of the screw to the instruments of torture I wore in my mouth, his fat secretary would give us a card bearing the date of my next appointment, and then we were free; everything bad was over; we could descend the stairs again to the varied joys of Copley Square, that triangular plaza with its quaternity of purveyors to the mind, spirit, body, and what one might perhaps call the worldly part of one's nature — the Public Library, Trinity Church, S. S. Pierce's, and the Copley Plaza.

Perhaps we would have an ice among the potted palms of the marble-floored Copley Plaza; perhaps we would wander farther down Boylston Street to get a chocolate ice-cream soda at Huyler's, passing on our way the statue of Phillips Brooks, the general style of whose sculpture was best summed up by the little Boston boy who said of the Christ looking over Brooks's shoulder, "Who is the lady, Mamma?" Sometimes we went to the Public Library, and I sat, with a book from the Children's Room, in one of the yellow marble niches on the stairway, facing the proud tablets to the Massachusetts Regiments that listed so many battles — Antietam, Fredericksburg, Bull Run — while my mother, up on the top floor, looked at reproductions of Chardin in the Art Department. But we always ended up, before it was time to catch our train at the Back Bay Station, by going in out of the gathering dusk to the brightly lighted, discreetly busy, delicious-smelling interior of S. S. Pierce's. This was not the main store, which was down among the encanyoned cow paths of the business section of town, but a branch; nevertheless for me, and I suspect for many, it *was* S. S. Pierce's.

On my left as we enter is the tobacco counter; while my mother hurries away to the rather undramatic grocery counter that runs the full length of the store to the right, I pause to admire the boxes of cigars, opened to display the beautiful shiny pictures, in gold and bright colors on the flaps, of heavily ringleted ladies, mustachioed gentlemen; and the long, neat tubes of tobacco within, each with its red-and-gold band. Elderly friends of my father's, when taking a Romeo y Julieta, used to be fond of slipping such a band upon my finger, solemnly affiancing me.

Beyond are the toilet things — toilet waters, and cans of talcum powder, and soaps. They slightly bore me, except for the boxes of Pears' soap, oval, translucent, and brown as a chestnut, which give me a pang of nostalgia for the summertime, when we go to my Aunt Ellen's on the North Shore; my Aunt Ellen uses no soap but Pears'. At the back of the store are the wines and spirits, which

I am willing to leave to others to admire; between me and them are the cheese cases, full of round red-rinded cheeses, cheeses like pineapples, moldy cheeses, great wheels of Stilton. A museum director once brought such a wheel as a present to my mother, but it got thrown out in the garbage the following day by the maid, Bridie, who thought it had gone bad, because of the maggots. But what I am heading for is the party-favor counter, slightly to the right of the entrance. It is not really a counter at all but a circular pyramidal structure with tiers, upon which are displayed miraculous confections of crepe paper and paper lace: little baskets for candy to put at each place at a party; multicolored snappers with shiny cardboard pictures affixed to them; place cards in the form of boats, flowers, animals; Jack Horner pies with a fountain of streamers gushing forth, attached to untold marvels hidden within; favors for cotillions, such as small white celluloid fans, enameled boxes, paper tiaras, miniature books with pictures of violets on the cover. I walk round and round this monument to gaiety, gravely inspecting each article, wanting them all; needing them all. All too soon my mother has finished giving her order for California pea beans and guava jelly, and we hurry out of the Dartmouth Street entrance into the cold Back Bay twilight and up over the bridge (under which a train sometimes passes as we cross, with the noise of a cataclysm and a deluge of smoke) to take our train for home, down in the strange, dark, echoing, coal-gaseous, windy, bitter-cold cavern of the Back Bay Station.

There was always a special aura to a box from S. S. Pierce's when one opened it — a japanned box of candied ginger for Christmas or, when I grew up to be a debutante and began to receive presents of circumscribed variety from beaux, a box of Pierce's own brand of cigarettes, in white, crisp, pristine packages. But the boxes I remember best opening were the boxes of peppermints from Pierce's that my mother took for a present to my Aunt Ellen when we went to visit her at the seashore; being a child, I was allowed to do the opening. First one removed the outside paper — white, tied with a twisted red-and-white string. Next one lifted the cover of the white box, with its familiar gold shield — the lion within it, the eagle above it. One then encountered a padding of quilted paper and, underneath, double flaps of crisp waxed paper, to be laid gently aside, exposing the top layer of peppermints — white, fragile, lying side by side without overlapping. There were many such layers to a pound box, each separated from the next by a sheet of waxed paper as delicately fresh as a petal; the whole had an aura at once formal, untouched, and delicious.

Since I have grown up, it has been my experience that other grocers, no matter how fancy, are apt to seem at first intriguing but in the end cold and foreign. I suppose that, like many a Boston lady who lives far nearer the water side of Beacon Street than I do, I feel that Pierce's understands me. When I go up, as I do, from Virginia to spend the summers in my late Aunt Ellen's old house, it is S. S. Pierce's who know that I have come without my notifying them — I suppose they have some sort of memorandum — and resume purveying to me for the months that I am there.

Every Saturday afternoon — late, for the delivery route is a long one — the high green Pierce's truck draws up by the side of the road and the Pierce's man comes climbing up the hill to the house, against a wild sunset background of sea and sky, the big wooden delivery box, with slot handles, balanced on his shoulder. There is a reassuring bang on the kitchen table as he sets the box down. "Pierce's!" he calls. I hurry out to the kitchen, to find him setting the different boxes and packages out on the table with small subsidiary bangs. Hearty, sweaty, robust, smiling — all Pierce's delivery men look alike — he will not stay to talk; he must get on. And, some Thursday late in September of each year, the telephone will ring as usual at about half past eight. "Good morning. S. S. Pierce," says the pleasant, businesslike voice at the other end. "I haven't any order to give you today," I have to say. "I'm going away next week." "Is that right?" says the voice. "Well, I hope you have a pleasant winter." But even when I am home in the South, I still feel in touch.

When I first came to live in Virginia, I was introduced at the houses of hospitable friends to all manner of choice delicacies new to me — tobacco-brown, pungent hams, spoon bread, tomatoes cooked down to a thick rich paste, eggnog that took a week to make, brandied peaches buried in the earth to strengthen; but one day I was invited to the house of a new acquaintance for tea. She lived in a tiny brick house behind one of the pavilions of the lawn of the University of Virginia; it had once been the servants' quarters, and was now as snugly arranged for living as a little satin-lined jewel box. Before a cannel-coal fire in a minute grate we sat down to a tea table laden with Dresden cups; a copper teakettle simmered over a candle flame. The tea was in a gold-colored canister with a red-and-white shield on it; on the curate's assistant were plates of buttered, toasted, paper-thin cassava cakes such as I had not seen since my childhood, and of what were surely Huntley & Palmers Digestive Biscuits. I stared at my hostess with a wild surmise. "Where —" I began. "My mother came from Boston," she said, following my eyes. "I send in a monthly order to Pierce's." She pronounced it "Perse's." This was the beginning of a long and lively friendship, the foundation of which seems to me to have been as good as any.

10

At one time, which was about the time of the first World War, everyone took the train to go to Boston. It took twenty-five minutes from the town we lived in. There were the 8:10, the 8:25, and the 8:45. These trains were known as the Workers', the Clerkers', and the Shirkers' among the men who traveled in the smoking car and read their morning newspapers in a haze of blue smoke, comfortably, as the train racketed through Hyde Park, West Roxbury, Spring Street, in to the South Station.

There was no train service during the middle of the day and when I was eight or nine and had to go once a week to Boston to have my teeth straightened, my mother took me on the streetcar, but afterward we walked up Boylston Street to the Back Bay Station and took one of the commuters' trains home again. The cars were hot and stuffy and lighted with yellow gas lamps on the ceiling. The brakeman came with a long pole to pull down the round glass shades that covered them, and then he hopped up on the wooden arm of a seat to light each one with a match. We sat on green or red plush seats which were gritty with cinders, and looked out from our warmth over the dark landscape flying by. Before we came to our town the train went across a long marsh, flat and unbroken under snow, and halfway across the bell would begin to ring on the engine and the train to slow for the station.

When we got out into the cold twilight, we usually took a cab home. There were two station cabs, and we always took Mr. Harvey's, because we were afraid that nobody else ever did. He was an old man with a long white beard. The other man, Mr. Mathews, was younger and had a big, drooping, tobacco-stained mustache and looked like a gambler in a melodrama. He stepped forward when the crowds got off the train, indicating his cab with one arm and repeating "Cab? Cab?" in a loud voice. He always got passengers and drove his horse away down the station drive even before the train had pulled out. He would take four or even five passengers and drop them off at their houses all over town.

But Mr. Harvey stood on the curb in the cold, silent. His horse, beside him, drooped its head. Mr. Harvey had owned his station cab since before Mr. Mathews came to the town, and it was far shabbier than Mr. Mathews's cab and his horse was slow. Sometimes, when we walked home from the station, I would look back and the platform would be empty and Mr. Harvey, in his old overcoat and ear-muffed cap, would be climbing up behind his horse to drive his empty cab away.

I hated Mr. Mathews. I wanted wildly to do something for Mr. Harvey, and there was nothing I could do. He had an old wife who was bedridden, and I used to have terrible pictures of his returning, late and cold and tired, and her voice saying "Anything?" and his replying "Nothing." I hoped they had enough to eat. I hoped that they were warm. I always smiled at him so hard it made my face hurt, hoping that perhaps it would make some difference to him.

My mother was sorry for him, too, and so we always had him when we needed a cab — to take my mother and father out to dinner, to take me to birthday parties. He would talk to us through the flapping black curtain that separated his seat from ours about how his wife was doing these days, about the way the town was changing. Mr. Mathews was doing so well that he did not need to go out into the cold to meet the late-night trains, but Mr. Harvey needed anything he could get, and so he met all the trains.

Once my mother and I had been away visiting my aunt and there was a severe snowstorm that made our train from New York to Boston very late. We caught the last train to our town and when we got out, the only passengers, there was Mr. Harvey standing by his horse in the silent, falling snow; in the night. He lifted our bags into the cab and drove us home through the strange, exciting, late streets. "It's real late for a little girl to be up," he said.

Once an extraordinary thing happened. He appeared at our front door with a necklace that his wife had made for me out of some gray, pearly, dried seeds, tied with a blue ribbon.

Mr. Mathews added another cab to his business. It was driven by his son Frank, a thin and pimply boy of about seventeen. Frank was even more enterprising than his father, pushing forward into the crowds and gesturing toward the two cabs, insisting "Cab? Cab?" Those cabs now had MATHEWS' LIVERY STABLE smartly painted on their sides. At about the time that Mr. Mathews introduced the first station automobile cab, which Frank Mathews drove, old Mr. Harvey died.

From that time we had to use the Mathews cabs. Mr. Mathews was growing old and did not know how to drive an automobile, so his son Frank, with his taxi, was in much more demand. Once I saw old Mr. Mathews saying something to him on the platform and heard Frank say "Shut up" as he sprang forward to attract a passenger. Pretty soon there were two automobiles, and the horse cab disappeared entirely from the station. Mr. Mathews just loafed around the men's waiting room, watching the trains come in and leave. Another boy of Frank's age drove the other taxi; MATHEWS' TAXI was now painted on the doors.

Frank seemed the perfect, successful, modern go-getter of the new times that had come. Once he drove me to a party. The taxi smelled just the same as the cabs had — of stable. The sliding window behind Frank's head was open and he talked to me as he drove about the liquor you could get if you knew where, about the big time the gang had at Moseley's Saturday nights. I didn't want to talk to him, and when he reached his arm through the window and opened the door for me at the house where I was going, he said, "Pretty snooty, aren't you, kid?"

Frank wore a black chauffeur's cap on one side of his head and raised his eyebrows knowingly at the girls at the station. His taxis were the only ones in town, and eventually there were four of them. I think by that time old Mr. Mathews was dead.

Before I grew up and left home, the rich men stopped going into Boston on the train and drove or were driven there in their own cars. The workers and the clerkers still went by train and so did the housewives who went in for a day's shopping, and when they came home tired, they took one of Mathews' taxis. At that time one of them was a Packard limousine, and Frank, who was fatter and older, drove this himself. The others were nice, smart, shiny sedan cars. The limousine was always used for funerals and weddings.

The last time I went back there I found that the turreted château which had been the station was boarded up and deserted, and old newspapers were blowing about its walls. The train service to Boston had been discontinued and the tracks were rusting. There was a dirty, scribbled-on FOR SALE sign nailed to the station, hopelessly, for who would buy a brownstone castle in the middle of a town, and for what?

A bus now ran every twenty minutes from the center of the town to Boston, a new red-and-yellow bus with comfortable seats. The old trolley tracks in the middle of Washington Street had been torn up. In the window of Mr. Tracy's news agency there was a printed card that said CALL MATHEWS' TAXI and at the curb in front of the store stood a limousine. I walked past and saw Frank Mathews there, behind the wheel. He was slumped down into a thick, rusty, black winter coat, his chauffeur's cap set straight and low over his eyes. He looked fat and unhealthy and as if he was used to sitting there inside his closed car all day. I nodded at him through the window of the car. He cranked the window down quickly and leaned across the seat.

"Well, you're quite a stranger," he said. "Run you up the hill?"

"No, thanks," I said. "I'm walking."

He ran the window up again and settled back. The limousine was several years out of date and I wondered if it still smelled, inside, of stable. The bus came purring up to a stop, just ahead at the corner; the folding door at the front opened and a party of school children got out and ran up the street toward the drugstore. They did not look back, and so it was impossible to tell whether any of them felt anything special about Frank Mathews and his old taxi, whether pity or contempt.

11

WHEN I WAS A CHILD, WE USED TO GO TWO OR THREE
times a year to lunch at my Uncle Paul's. We always
went on my birthday, because it was his birthday, too,
and he always remembered it and asked us. The birthday came early in June, and for dessert we would have
ice cream and, on top, the strawberries that Uncle Paul
raised. He raised them as one of his hobbies. They were
the biggest strawberries I had ever seen, dark red and
juicy, as big as small plums.

My Uncle Paul had never married. My father said
that he had always been too shy even to call on girls. He
was born about 1870. When I knew him, he was sturdy
and plump and very well dressed. He had pink cheeks
and his gray hair was cut very neatly. He was very hospitable and gentle. He lived in a house in the country
just outside our town, with two Irish maids. The cook
cooked very good food and the waitress wore a white
cap and used to smile at me when she passed the things.

Uncle Paul had studied to be an architect. He went to

the Beaux-Arts in Paris and stayed over there about ten years, all through the nineties. He lived on the Rue des Saints-Pères on the Left Bank, in a house with other students at Julian's and the Beaux-Arts. He must have had a very good time in his own gentle way, because long afterward, when I knew him, all his little stories were about Paris.

One of them was about an American who had just come to Paris to study and lived in the same house with Uncle Paul. This American had asked the concierge to bring him up some hot water to shave with. The water didn't come, and the American went to the head of the stairs and bawled down, *"Voulez-vous apporter moi l'eau chaude ou voulez-vous non?"*

In Paris, my Uncle Paul used to see most of the famous artists who were there in those days. He used to see Whistler and Monet, and once he saw Wilde, who was then in the evil days before his death. Uncle Paul said that later in Paris there was a society formed of people who had admired Wilde's work and who claimed that he was not dead but living somewhere still. They claimed that no one had seen him in his coffin and that what Lord Alfred Douglas said did not count. When I knew my Uncle Paul first, it was at least 1915, and he used to say then and later that perhaps Wilde was still not dead.

Uncle Paul had never practiced as an architect. The only thing he ever designed which was built after he came back to America was the house he lived in. This was a white, shingled house of an Early American type, very neat and trim outside, and inside very comfortable. The house was just like him. There was a lawn in the front and a big lawn in back that you looked out on from the living room, with a fishpond in the middle. Beyond that lay the vegetable gardens. My Uncle Paul had a gardener to help him, and he raised strawberries and green-flesh melons and other specialties that won blue ribbons at the Grange fairs. He had enough money, so he had never needed to work, and he just lived there in his nice house that exactly suited him.

Beyond the gardens were the pinewoods. They ran back for a long way, and it was very dark in among the pines and the roof of the treetops was far up above. When we went to lunch with Uncle Paul, I would go out into the woods and play, building a tepee out of pine branches leaned against a tree trunk. I only got a little done each time, and we did not go very often, but nobody ever moved the part I had done, so I would go on with it the next time I went.

The others would stroll around across the lawns and through the gardens while I was in there in the secret pinewoods. Once, when I was about thirteen, my Uncle Paul came into the tepee, where I was, and stood and watched me fixing the boughs. (I always imagined at home that it was much more of a structure than it really was, and I was always disappointed when I got there and found only some branches leaning against a tree, letting in light and air, when I had thought of it as a tight place where I could go inside and be as snug as if I were in a house.) I felt someone standing behind me and turned around, and it was my Uncle Paul. He had a little gray mustache on his pink face and he was dressed, as always, in a nice, warm, brown suit of tweeds. He showed me a way to fix the branches so that they would interlock and stand much more firmly against the tree.

"I want it to be so I can get inside and be safe," I said.

"You always have to leave a door," he said. "You can have it all shut in except that."

After a while he walked away. He never bothered people. He had these pleasant lunch parties that gave pleasure to the guests, with splendid, rich desserts the children liked, and everybody had a good time. He never asked you too often — just often enough so that you were glad to go again.

During the first World War, my Uncle Paul gave a good deal of money to the Allied Relief, my father said, and he used to knit washcloths for the soldiers. When we went to lunch there, it was just the same, except that the gardener had gone to the war and Uncle Paul knitted washcloths after lunch. The food was a little different, because we all had to do without wheat and sugar and such things. But it was still good, plentiful food and he always had the same cook and waitress.

I used to think that my Uncle Paul had the best life of anyone I had ever heard of. He had been born just at the right time to be out of any bad trouble in the world. He had never married anybody and he lived alone in just the way that he chose and he did not have to work or be with people except when he asked them to come. He was very shy and I understood about that. Once there was a dinner for old Beaux-Arts men and my Uncle Paul had to go to it. He was in a panic for fear he might have to speak, and he could not eat any dinner. But in the end he did not have to speak at all. Nothing had ever happened to him, nothing, nothing. He was able to live his life and enjoy it without being troubled by all the things that tortured other people — debt and worry and misunderstanding and fights. He could live his life and enjoy it as it passed day by day and nothing happened.

But later on, when I was grown-up, my Uncle Paul began to have heart trouble. He would have frightful attacks of pain quite suddenly when he was going upstairs or even sitting in a chair.

He was beside himself with terror. I don't know what he was afraid of, whether it was the pain itself or whether it was the fear of dying. He got a doctor to come and live with him in the house. His name was Dr. Alexander. He was a short man with an olive complexion and smooth black hair. He called my Uncle Paul

"Paul," but Uncle Paul, who was a formal man, always called him "Dr. Alexander." Dr. Alexander lived in Uncle Paul's house from that time on.

My mother and father still went there to lunch a few times a year, but I had gone away from home then and I did not see my Uncle Paul for a long time. I still thought of him as having the best life I had ever seen lived. I was sorry that his heart had gone bad, but when I thought of him, I saw the smooth, green lawns and the specimen strawberries like great ruby blobs among the green leaves, and the comfortable chintz-covered chairs in the living room, and everything beautifully neat and orderly and nothing happening.

Once, though, I went to lunch there again when I was visiting at home. It was different. It did not seem to be Uncle Paul's house any more but to belong to Dr. Alexander. Dr. Alexander was a sociable man and he did all the talking at lunch and my Uncle Paul sat silent. Dr. Alexander talked about operations he had seen performed. After lunch we walked out on the lawn in back of the house, where a putting green had been arranged so that Dr. Alexander could practice shots. Of course, no one could have said that Dr. Alexander was anything but nice to my Uncle Paul. But he was an active man and he liked things to happen, and so he kept the conversation going gaily and kept jumping up and lighting cigarettes and everything was different. He kept talking about his days in the hospital, and when he started saying anything about the present, he would begin, "You know, we lead a very quiet life here. Poor Paul . . ." Uncle Paul hardly spoke during the time we were there at lunch. He looked frightened. It was not his house any more and he was frightened about his heart and he could not do without Dr. Alexander.

About a year after I lunched there, my Uncle Paul died. I was told he had had a bad attack when he was lying on the sofa after dinner and it was so agonizing that he was screaming; he rolled off the sofa in his anguish and it was on the floor that he died. He left all his money to Dr. Alexander. I do not know what Dr. Alexander has done with it or where he is living now.

12

THERE WAS A DANCING SCHOOL IN OUR TOWN IN THOSE days to which all the same children that went to the day school went on Thursday afternoons. Dancing school kept only through the four most wintry months, and all the girls took their slippers in slipper bags, to put on after they had pulled off their snowy galoshes. They were the same children as at regular school, but something about that dancing school, something about that difficult, festive, late-afternoon atmosphere made me feel twice as shy of them and twice as left out as at day school.

The class was held in Odd Fellows' Hall, down in the village — a severe, ugly, brick building beyond the post office. *Odd Fellows' Hall* was printed in old gilt letters on a big board made of a sort of black sandpaper, over the door. You went up a steep, straight flight of stairs to the second floor, your best dress enveloped by your heaviest coat, in your ice-flecked galoshes and the woolen stockings that would be peeled off in the cloakroom. Already you could hear the notes of quick, disquieting music played on a piano — "Babes in the Wood" or the "Merry Widow Waltz." Coats were taken off in a dark room full of long racks, and at the door to the big hall you mixed in the confused crowd that was forming into a double column to march in. There was a queer, tremulous feeling about being in your best dress, in your patent-leather ankle-ties; your legs felt long and cold in unaccustomed thin stockings.

The lady that played the piano played it very loud and fast and brightly. When she dashed into the beginning of the "Radetsky March," that meant that we were to come in. Two by two, girl and boy and girl and boy, we would march down the length of the hall to where Miss Macomber stood in turquoise-blue taffeta, cut short enough to show her beautiful little feet in bronze kid slippers with high heels. Although I can remember all the rest of it, I can never remember what her face was like. All I remember is the turquoise dress she always wore and those small, intelligent feet in bronze pumps. At the end of the procession there were always two or three couples of girls, because there were never enough boys to go around. I was usually at the end.

Coming into the room was like bursting into some strange and alarming paradise, some enchanted place where you did not belong. The floor was vast and shining; far down at the end stood the piano on a platform, with the lady's hands lifting and dropping on the keys;

and Miss Macomber, little and straight and formal, bowing to each couple as they bowed and curtsied and went to the gilt chairs along the wall.

Miss Macomber had a high, clear voice, and she used to call the dances and tell us what to do, as we sat along the wall in the small, fragile gilt chairs that seemed so elegant. We sat with our ankles crossed, and anybody who forgot and dangled her legs was quickly corrected across the floor by Miss Macomber, who never forgot anyone's name. There were short pauses between the dances, when the music stopped and Miss Macomber would walk, with her little delicate steps, across to the chairs where the mothers sat, and talk to them. The children whispered and laughed across each other, and squirmed in their seats; there was a very special hush in the air between dances. The lights, the big brass chandeliers in the ceiling, were always on in those winter afternoons, although when we first came in, the western sun shone in through the windows that looked over the courthouse, and mixed with the false light.

Then the hush would break with a snap as Miss Macomber tap-tapped across the floor and called out, "Boys, choose your partners for the Slide Polka," or, "Form two lines for practice in the Waltz." Then everyone would lumber forward, awkwardly, half giggling, and the music would begin, gay and important and foreign-sounding.

There were girls that were always chosen for partners,

and there were girls who generally had to dance together unless Miss Macomber did some arranging. The clumsy ones were sometimes picked to dance with Miss Macomber herself. That was like flying. Her hand lay very lightly, very surely, on the back of your dress, and you felt yourself dancing, really dancing, round and round. Sometimes I danced with other heavy, lumbering girls, and sometimes Miss Macomber took a boy, in his blue serge suit, and held him by the arm and brought him up to where I sat; then, according to formula, he would bow — a jerk of the head and shoulders that made his hair flop in his eyes — and mumble, "M'ave pleasuris dance?"

But I always liked it best when I had been doing two-steps all wrong, finding it impossible to make the little double-step at the turns, and Miss Macomber would put her arm around my shoulders and dance with me herself. Anyone could have flown with her. Somehow, when I danced with her, I felt I belonged here, that I had some actual part in it all, and I never felt that at any other time.

In the intervals between the dances, when the other children were whispering, I used to look at the hall we were in, and at the faint and fading glow that came in the windows of the west. It was so hushed; the room full of people seemed to become projected and remote, as if it floated; everyone was quite still, even the lady at the piano; everyone sat still and whispered. Outside the red sun hung above the white horizon, and the streets were cold and white, leading back into the country where I lived, and where the drifts were deep and purple-shadowed as the sun went down.

I used to look at the strange pictures painted on the walls. Each wall had a round medallion painted high up near the ceiling; one of a huge ear; one of a mouth; one of a red and bleeding heart; and one of an enormous, wide-open eye; all painted with terrible lifelike detail — the red shadows of the ear, the pupil of the eye. I used to wonder why they were painted there.

At the end of each dancing class we formed for the Grand March, and paraded two by two around the room to the fast and stirring march music; we formed fours, separated, formed eights, fours, twos, and by ones marched round and round into a spiral from which the leader had to extricate us. Finally the march to Miss Macomber to bow and curtsy good-by; we tramped up to her tiny, erect figure and fumbled through the gestures, and marched again out of the door to the cloakroom.

It was all over. Coats and galoshes were put on again, and you went down those steep stairs to the dark street where street lamps shone on the heaped-up snow, your slipper bag in your hand. The magic, the queer loneliness and unbearable feeling of not belonging, the bright, foreign atmosphere were over, and I used to walk back with my mother along the frozen, rutted roads, in the darkness, into the round radiance of a country street-light and into the darkness again.

It was in a February that I went on the wrong day. I knew it as soon as I opened the big door and climbed the stairs — there was no music, and no sounds of chattering. I had a hard pang of hurt because I knew nobody well enough to learn such a thing as the others would, by passed-around word of mouth. I wished hard, as I often wished, that we didn't live far out in the country, but in one of the warm, snug little houses in the village, where I would be one of the crowd; and then right off I knew, as I always knew, that that wouldn't make the difference I wanted, that it was something else, that there was just something wrong with me.

I went on climbing the stairs, slowly, and an old man came out from the cloakroom and said, "Hello." He looked at me, and I came on upstairs and stood there, not wanting to go home after I had walked to the village to go to dancing school.

"Guess you didn't hear, school's put off till next week. Lady's sick," he said. He went on looking at me, amiably. I knew he must be the caretaker. He had on an old overcoat and a cap with ear muffs, and he was smoking a pipe.

"What are those pictures for in the hall? What do they mean?" I asked him, swinging my slipper bag.

"Them? They're part of the Odd Fellows, y'know. I didn't ought to give away what they mean."

"Oh," I said. I started to go downstairs again.

"Want to see the stuff they rig up in?" he asked suddenly. I went upstairs again. I didn't know what he meant. He opened some big wardrobe cupboards beyond the rows of racks. I had never noticed the cupboards, beyond the mess of children's coats that always hung in front when I came.

There were scarlet robes trimmed with ermine, and purple robes, and great cloaks of velvet and satin and plush and fur. There were gold crowns and great high headdresses studded with huge jewels. There were satin suits in brilliant colors, and jeweled scepters stacked in a corner.

"The Odd Fellows, they rig up in these here when they hold their meetings," he said. "A fine sight."

I looked past the wardrobes to the long, empty hall, with its floor shining in the western sunlight. I could see them all, dressed like kings and princes, holding court in the hall. At last I knew why there was a throne at the end of the room, beside the piano where the lady played for dancing; the greatest king of all sat in it, and all the gorgeous others sat about in the gilded chairs, in their scarlet and purple and ermine. That was what this hall was for. This was its real meaning, not a children's dancing class. I saw them, glittering in their magnificence under the artificial lights, under the shining chandeliers, holding their strange and magnificent rites.

He showed me all the things, and then he shut up the wardrobes and I went away, down the stairs into the cold late-afternoon street. I walked home through the winter dusk, thinking about the Odd Fellows and wondering who they were. Did they meet secretly here, coming from far spots all over the earth to hold their gorgeous meetings in a building deceptively brick and ugly? I thought about them as you would think about a wonderful rich secret — I had seen their robes and their finery; I knew about their meetings. Nobody else did.

None of the other children, having their dancing class, whispering and laughing and owning the place, knew that this place was the scene of magnificent revels. Nobody but me. It was a hot, vibrating feeling inside me. Now, suddenly, I belonged and nobody else did. I knew a secret about the Odd Fellows' Hall.

Afterwards I used to think about the royal robes that were hidden so near, as I sat on the gilt chairs and listened to the quick dance music starting up. I always had a proprietary sense, secretly; a realization that I knew the real meaning of the place. I never felt so left out, after that.

13

It was a hot summer, and the tar on the road between my house and the Welch children's house was always soft and sticky, and you could smell it in the mornings. The bees sang in the syringa bush, and around the corner of our house there were humming-birds in the hollyhocks. The grass burned yellow on the front lawn early in the summer, and the cicadas shrilled in the yellow, burning meadows, and at the end of June we were all taken to the circus in town on a very hot day.

We were sent with Miss Perkins, the Welch chil-dren's governess. They had no mother and Mr. Thomp-son Welch could never go to things like that because he was an important lawyer. My mother and my father were always busy painting; they often felt guilty about me and took me to things like circuses, but really they wanted to paint, and the governess was the solution. There were Tom Welch and Royal Welch, and Jinny and May, in that order. The two girls were dressed just alike, although they were two years apart, and the boys' clothes were also alike. Mr. Welch ordered everything for them in big batches once or twice a year.

It was terribly hot at the circus under the tent, and like a dream. We all stuck together and the governess did not get in the way; it was as good as if she had not been there. We each had fifty cents to buy things with; I had found out how much the Welch children were going to have to spend and asked for the same. My dress was almost like the Welch girls', too. We all wore striped gingham dresses, the stripes running up and down, and a belt loose around our hips. The Welch boys wore knickers and white shirts and carried their coats. We stayed through the big show and wanted to stay for the Buffalo Bill Wild West Show, but the governess said we would not get home in time for supper.

We still had some of our money left after pop and Cracker Jack and peanuts, which we had fed to the elephants in the menagerie before the show began. We wandered slowly out of the tent with the moving crowd. There was a man with a big board in front of him; on the board lizards were chained — greenish, goldish, brownish lizards. We all stopped in front of the lizard man and he showed us how the lizards would change color when you put them against things of different colors. They were called chameleons, the governess said. Jinny and May and I each bought one and the boys each bought two, and that made seven lizards we had to take home with us.

The day after the circus, my mother made me stay in bed. I felt as if I were somewhere else, watching myself, and my father said I had a touch of sunstroke from the heat at the circus. I kept my lizard beside my bed in a box cover filled with sand. Around his neck he had a little gold chain with a gold pin on the end of it, and the pin was attached to the edge of the box cover. There was also a saucer filled with water with sugar in it, and the water was less by evening, so he must have taken some of it. But I could not see that he was drinking. He lay perfectly still in the sand most of the time, and then his head would twitch as quick as lightning from side to side, and he would dart forward on his lizard legs, and flash his head to the sides, and again be perfectly still, without even a tremor.

I stayed in bed all day with the shades drawn halfway down, and outside the day roared and blazed and glared its length. That night there was a thunderstorm just after sunset. When the storm went away, it was still raining a little, a cool, quiet rain, and the air that came in my windows smelled cool and freshened. The next morning, when I woke up, I felt all right. It had started in being hot again, and the sound of the cicadas went higher and higher into the orange sunlight from the meadows, and I could see my father painting over in the field beyond the swamp, far away. I could see the shape of the canvas on the easel and the figure sitting behind it, a spot of white with a white dot at the top. That was the old pith helmet he always wore out in the sun to paint. The meadows were hot and murmuring with bees and insects, and after breakfast I went over to the Welches' house.

The Welch children were all down behind the stone wall at the back of their house, on their hands and knees. They had built an enclosure with stones, about four feet square, that backed up against the stone wall.

"We've got a lizard farm," Royal said. He had invented it. He invented most of the things we did. They had a hole dug and a bowl fitted into it for sugar water for the lizards. The lizard farm was in the shade, except for one corner where the sunlight fell through the leaves. I went and got my lizard from home and put him in. We tied long strings around their necks instead of the golden chains, so that the lizards would have room to move around, and tied the strings to rocks.

"They're not at home yet," Royal said. "We have to keep them tied up until they get used to it. Then we can let them loose and they'll live here."

We played all day with the lizard farm, making a shelter where the lizards could go when it rained and a small hillock to climb when they wanted to see out over the rock wall we had built. The lizards lay on their stomachs, and once in a while one of them would dart around a little, or another would look from side to side almost instantaneously. We built up the lizard farm so it had every convenience we could think of. We caught flies and put them in front of the lizards, but they did not eat the dead flies. The lizards were inert, and yet you felt that they were ready to dart at any moment. Building things that they would like made us feel as if we were getting to know them better. It was hard to know how a lizard felt. They were secret and mysterious, not like other animals.

"If we watch them every day, we will get to understand them," Royal said. "We will get to know the habits of lizards. Then we can teach them tricks."

"What kind of tricks?" Jinny asked.

"We won't know what kind of tricks till we know what lizards are like," he said. "We have to know what lizards are capable of."

The next day, in the morning, we went back to the lizards. They were just the same, still inscrutable, but the sugar water was all gone.

"Let's have a fair," Royal said, "and exhibit our performing lizards at it."

"But they can't perform yet," I said. "We don't understand them yet."

"We'll understand them by that time. By that time we will have taught them a few simple tricks."

We were always planning fairs. We would do things — learn to do new tricks on the Welches' trapeze or make some candy that turned out well — and our successes would come to a kind of head, and we would decide to have a fair. We had never had any of them, but we were sincere about it. Each time we really meant this time to have a fair. We would get far into the plans, deciding how much admission we would ask, and what kind of booths there would be, and how much money we would clear from it, and what the money would be spent for. This was the first fair we had planned that summer, and we decided to have it in Mrs. French's barn. We would have lemonade and a candy booth and a fancy-articles booth and a grab bag and a pin-the-tail-on-the-donkey, and May would sit in her pink dress and take ten-cent admissions. We saw it all very clearly, the crowd milling about and ourselves very busy, attending to everything. And in the middle there would be a booth with Royal in it, exhibiting the performing lizards.

"I can give all my time to training them between now and the fair," he said. "We'll have to put up placards on the telephone poles saying about the fair, and the rest of you'll have to make all the placards and the fancy articles, and get everything ready. And somebody will have to ask Mrs. French. And we'll have to make the tickets for admission and everything."

For several days we talked about the fair all the time —to the Welches' governess, whom we always told about our fairs, and to my mother and father, who always made good suggestions. And the Welches must have told their father.

I saw Mr. Welch seldom. He was a slim, well-dressed

man with a clean-shaven upper lip that bulged out, and he was very efficient about his four children and ran them like a business. He always left tasks for the children to get done during the week, while he was in town, and they always did them before they got around to anything else. He often gave talks to his children when they were rounded up and sitting in chairs in the living room. After one of his talks, the Welch household would run unnaturally for a while, with the children talking about their tasks — a word my parents never used — and about responsibility. Then the normal atmosphere would creep back into the Welch house and they would all be the way they really were, Tom serious and slow, Royal excited about a new idea and using long words in explaining it, Jinny passionate and intense about everything, and May pretty and silly.

One evening I had been home from the Welches' for some time, and had had supper, and was up in my room writing in my private book. The frogs were very loud outside in the swamp and my father was playing Chopin on our piano. The music suddenly stopped and I heard my father get up and walk across the floor downstairs. I heard his voice and my mother's voice and Mr. Welch's voice. I put down my private book and listened.

I thought perhaps I had done something that had made Mr. Welch mad, because he seldom came over to our house. I thought perhaps he had come to complain about me. I walked in my bare feet to the top of the stairs and sat down with my feet on the step below. The lights were out upstairs and I sat in the dark and listened. The door to the study, where they sat, was open.

"Look here," Mr. Welch said. "You know these fairs the children are always planning? Well, I learn that they're planning a new one. Miss Perkins tells me they've been planning it for days."

"I've heard a little about it," my mother said.

"They can't be permitted to go on making these plans and never carrying them through," Mr. Welch said.

"Oh, see here, now," my father said. "That's part of it, just planning and nothing happening, you know."

"They must be taught that they must carry through what they plan. They'll never be competent to complete anything they undertake if they fall into the way of letting everything slide. They must be made —"

My father got up and walked across the floor and shut the living-room door. That was all I was able to hear. I sat there for a while, moving my toes on the cool boards of the stairs in the darkness, and then I went back in my room and went on writing in my private book.

The next morning, when I went over to the Welches', they were all being the efficient way and it wasn't any fun. Instead of lying out on the grass in the sun and drinking sarsaparilla and watching the lizards for hours, they were all doing tasks. Miss Perkins was supervising.

It was all busy and horrid. Mr. Welch had gone to see Mrs. French, and she had agreed to let us use her barn, and Mr. Welch had set the day, ten days ahead, when we had to have it. Royal was sitting at the desk in the living room painting posters with water colors. They said:

FAIR

At Mrs. French's Barn

July 16

2 to 6

COME ONE COME ALL

Admission, 25¢

Grab Bag

A Pony to Ride

Candy   Cakes   Drinks

Articles the Children Have Made

Mr. Welch had written down what the posters were to say. He had said that he would get the pony for the fair but that we must be responsible for the other things. Jinny was printing and cutting out tickets from green cardboard. May was making a pincushion out of pink silk. They gave me the first posters that were done, and I went down the road in the blazing sunshine with a hammer and tacks and fastened them to the telephone poles.

When I went home for lunch, my father was out in the back yard painting on an old barn door that had been lying about in the back of the barn for years. He had painted a double-life-size picture of the Kaiser on it, with an enormous round mouth under the pointed mustache, wide open. He stood there in the sun, walking up to the picture and walking away from it, putting on touches.

"Is that for the fair?" I asked.

He turned and made a face at me. "That's right," he said. "The mouth's going to be cut out so they can throw balls through it, five cents a throw. Old Welchy's idea."

I knew then that he had been forced into working for the fair just the way I had and that he thought it was boring and silly, too. But at lunch my mother said it would be fun. She said it would be very gay and that we would make some money to spend and that we would all have a good time. Even so, I knew she didn't think so. I knew my mother and father hated the whole idea and had been got into it by Mr. Welch and were bored and uncomfortable. But they couldn't say that to me. They had to stay on Mr. Welch's side.

We all worked hard for the fair, but the grown-up people did the most, because so many things came up that had never occurred to us when we were planning fairs. The day came, and we all ran around in the morning and were busy and got in the way. My mother got a carpenter to put up trestles for booths, and the whole inside of Mrs. French's barn was cleared out, dim and large. The booths were set around and things were put in them: candy, including some fudge that Jinny and I had made, and cakes made by our maid and the Welches' cook, and gallons of lemonade and grape juice and ginger ale mixed, and a booth of things that looked suddenly very odd when put out in public — the pink silk pincushion, and some cigar boxes Jinny had pasted pictures all over, and then a lot of our own things that we had desperately added at the last moment: Jinny's scrapbook and Tom's collection of postcards from all over the world and my scent bottle with the china-flower top. They were not all things we had made, but there was the sign THINGS THE CHILDREN HAVE MADE above it just the same. By noon we were all dressed up in our best clothes and running around and being told what to do by the grown-up people.

It was really an occasion. The people from the town began to come up the hill and along the road to Mrs. French's. At the entrance to her driveway there was a big sign that said:

THE CHILDREN'S FAIR
25¢
Proceeds to Charity

There had been some sort of row about that sign, but I did not know exactly what. Mr. Welch asked my father to paint it, and he refused when he found what Mr. Welch wanted written on it. My father painted a sign to use for the fair. It just had a big word FAIR on it and a picture of a little boy running fast. But that sign was stuck now over the barn door, where it did not matter. The big sign at the entrance was just printed, without pictures, and Tom had made it, painting on a big board with house paint.

The people straggled up the drive and into the barn. Just outside the barn door my father's picture of the Kaiser was set up, with the mouth cut open and a sign over it saying SOCK THE KAISER — 5¢. Balls were provided, and you got three shots to try to get one through the mouth, and it was very popular. Beside it stood Mr. Welch, calling attention to it. He was dressed for the fair in a pair of checked trousers and waistcoat, shirt sleeves, and a derby hat on the back of his head. He looked very strange. He stood there and called out, "Step right up here! Only five cents to give the Kaiser a socko! Step right up!"

I knew that he was trying to be like one of the side-show men at the circus, but somehow he embarrassed me, and I didn't look at him any more than I could help. But crowds came around him and lots of ladies just stood and talked to him and laughed and did not even try to sock the Kaiser. I was inside at the cake booth. Nobody seemed to want to buy cake on such a hot day. The cakes made me feel sick when I looked at them, they were so warm and rich and sticky. Two were chocolate, one was spice, and the rest had white frosting, so you could not tell what was inside. There were also cupcakes and cookies. I had a palm-leaf fan to wave away any flies. I wore my gray linen dress with a yellow sash woven in and out of slots, and my feet hurt, and I stood first on one and then on the other and smiled at the people who from time to time came up and peered at the cakes.

Tom had the candy booth and May was helping my mother sell the drinks. Jinny was behind the booth with the THINGS THE CHILDREN HAVE MADE sign. We waved at each other across the barn sometimes and smiled importantly. Royal was outside with the pony. The smallest children liked that best, and Royal, who was a tall boy, lifted them on and led the pony down to the brook and back again for five cents. Inside the dim barn I could see the pony pass by at intervals with Royal leading him.

At first it was all hectic and bewildering, and then it settled down, and I had time to look at the people. Later on it was just hot and sticky. The people began to thin out about five. By six, everyone had gone except a little boy who wanted to keep riding the pony, and Mr. Welch sent him home. It had clouded over and the atmosphere was heavy and misty. We all stood around tired and aimless. My mother looked hot and as if she were thinking about something else. My father, who had managed the grab bag until it was emptied, stood and mopped his forehead with his handkerchief. It looked stormy in the west.

Mr. Welch was still brisk and executive. He got the money from everybody and put it all together in one cigar box and began to count it. In between counting he gave orders: for Jinny to clear away the leftover things and put them all in a packing box, for Royal to take the pony back to the stable, for May to sweep up the barn floor, which was covered with litter.

"We must leave everything quite tidy," he said. "Mrs. French has been very kind."

He went on counting the money. My mother and my father sat down on a booth together and began to talk. I went to the door of the barn and watched the black clouds in the west rising. Mr. Welch shut the top of the cigar box and wrote something on a piece of paper and put it in his pocket. He stood up, in his checked trousers, with the hat on the back of his head; he still looked fresh and efficient.

"Eighteen dollars and ninety-two cents," he said. "That's not bad at all, is it?"

My father shrugged his shoulders.

"I'll just take it in charge," Mr. Welch said, "to give to my good friend Jimmy Stout."

"Why should you give it to your good friend Jimmy Stout?" my father asked.

"My dear chap," Mr. Welch said, "Jimmy Stout happens to be on the board of the Wanderers' Home. A splendid charity, and I believe I know all the board members."

"I'm sure you do," my father said. "But I understand the children want to give it to the Animal Rescue League, seeing they have to give it to something, which wasn't their idea, if you will remember."

"I think it had best be left to me," Mr. Welch said. "The Wanderers' is a very prominent charity, and I am sure all the board members will be touched that a group of children banded together to make it for them."

"Very useful," my father said. "Very helpful."

Mr. Welch looked at my father as if he didn't like to be told that it was useful or helpful. The sky was growing much darker, the sudden, unnatural darkness before a thunderstorm.

"We can't leave a matter of money to the children themselves," Mr. Welch said. "They are not equipped to handle money. I can assure you that I will see that this money is put to an excellent use."

"I have no doubt of it," my father said. I looked at him, for he seldom sounded as mad as he did now. "Seeing that nothing has been left to the children themselves, why should the proceeds be? After all —"

My mother pulled my father's sleeve. Mr. Welch put a broad elastic band around the cigar box and slipped it under his arm.

"Well," he said brightly, "I think it has all been very charming, very successful. The children are to be congratulated. Jinny, May, you mustn't forget that the cleaning up is yet to be done. Tomorrow there will be tasks for you. We must make everything look just as it did before all you children overran good Mrs. French."

Suddenly the storm broke. There was a splitting crash and the rain came down — hard, silver lines against the purply black of the atmosphere. The lightning darted down the west in an instantaneous blinding zigzag. Everyone clustered just inside the barn door. The rain washed down the picture of the Kaiser my father had painted, and already it looked like something from a long time ago that was over. Inside the barn it was hot and stuffy, but at the door I felt the cool freshness of the new air the storm had brought.

"We must make a dash for it," Mr. Welch said. He led off, running toward the Welches' house in his long, checked trousers, the rain soaking his shirt, and his children running after him. Our family waited in the barn.

"Was it pretty bad, old girl?" my father said to me.

"Oh, it was fun," I said. He looked at me for a moment and smiled.

"Real exploitation," he said to my mother.

The rain slackened a little and the thunder was farther away now, and I and my mother and my father walked home along the road to our house, not very fast.

By that time it was certainly a week since any of us had been down to the lizard farm or thought of the lizards at all. After the fair there was all that cleaning up for a day or two, and then one morning I went over to

138

the Welches', and they were all lying in the grass down where we had built the lizard farm. Tom and May were chewing grass. It was another hot day, and now everything was back where it had been. There was no more efficiency and they were just lying around in the grass. I dropped down too and leaned over on my elbows to look at the lizards.

There was only one visible. He lay quite still, and once in a while his head would twitch.

"The others have escaped," Royal said. "We found two of them dead — they smelled and we put them down the W.C. I don't know where the others have got to by now."

There were the six strings lying limp across the dirt inside the lizard farm. At the end of each string was an empty loop.

"It's the survival of the fittest," Royal said. "You see, this shows that this lizard is highly equipped to get along fine here. He likes it. I'm going to begin teaching him a few simple tricks."

He leaned over the lizard, poking him gently with a straw, but the lizard did not move. Only, from time to time, he would jerk his head like a flash. I lay on my back looking at the sky.

"We could put up a little booth by the roadside," Royal said, "and I could exhibit my performing lizard."

"How much would you charge?" Tom asked.

"Five cents a performance," Royal said.

"We could make lots and lots of money in a few weeks," Jinny said. "We could make enough to buy a canoe, and then we could go canoeing on the river, if we could get permission to go on the river."

"We could give it to the Little Wanderers," May said. "The poor Little Wanderers, who have no home or parents."

Jinny sat up straight in the grass.

"Are you going to the Macomber Dancing School in Boston next winter?" she asked me. She smoothed her black hair behind her ears and pursed her lips. "We're going to the Macomber Dancing School next year."

"I don't know," I said.

"I bet you aren't," Jinny said. "It's terribly hard to get into the Macomber Dancing School. We're going."

14

I SEE BY AN ADVERTISEMENT IN A YEAR-OLD MAGAZINE
I came across cleaning out my Virginia cellar that a big
hotel chain has bought the old Copley Plaza in Boston
and renamed it the Sheraton Plaza. This seems to me
absurd. It was called the Copley Plaza because it is on
Copley Square. My own early life was so bound up with
the Copley Plaza that I feel now very much as if someone insisted that I call my mother Mrs. Sheraton.

My earliest Copley Plaza memory is, I think, of Miss
Macomber's Boston dancing class, to which I went when
I was about twelve. No, from even before that there are
echoes: whispers of the small stringed orchestra playing
among the palms as I sit with my feet dangling above
the marble floor and am treated to an ice — raspberry or
orange — and something called *petits fours*. I have been
taken to a matinee to see, from a box, John Craig and
Mary Young do *Romeo and Juliet* at the Arlington
Street Theatre. The orchestra is playing a waltz called
"Les Patineurs," and the *petits fours* are beautiful —

green, pink, and white; diamond-shaped and square — but why "fours"? Because there are four corners, or what? I sit comfortably munching, and looking with favor at the palmy scene before me: this, then, is the great world, and very nice.

But by the time I began to go to Miss Macomber's some faint glaze of social comparisons had obscured my consciousness, and I was aware that Miss Macomber's was not the last word in Boston dancing classes. The last word was Foster's classes, held at the Somerset, out on Commonwealth Avenue.

Was it this that lent such a poignant, somehow heart-breaking quality to those late afternoons? Outside, the street lights are being turned on in the early-falling dusk along Dartmouth Street, Huntington Avenue, St. James Avenue. Inside the vast, marble, worldly Copley Plaza, the little girls are having their pink taffeta and blue satin sashes retied in the dressing room down the corridor from the ballroom. The moment comes, and we edge out into the corridor, where the boys wait in their blue serge suits. With somebody (who?) directing us, we form couples to march up the steps and into the smaller ballroom, where Miss Macomber, whom I had known when she taught a dancing class in the country, stands awaiting us in a peacock-blue taffeta dress and bronze kid slippers. The lady at the piano is playing "Won't You Wait Till the Cows Come Home?" We mince or shamble across the shining parquet; the boys bow, the girls curtsy, and then we hurry, with relief, away to reassemble strictly according to sex on the gilt chairs along the wall, until Miss Macomber gives the order "Boys, choose partners for the Slide Polka." At one end of the room, a few mothers sit — my mother among them — in their furs, their dark-blue suits neatly fitted over the bust, their plumed hats. Because of the tragic, romantic air of the whole thing, it is a relief to me when it is over and I am taken across Dartmouth Street, on our way home, to S. S. Pierce's, its lights blazing out in the Back Bay twilight, where I can walk round and round the circular display counter covered with party favors while my mother sits ordering California pea beans and a five-pound stone crock of strawberry jam at the grocery counter.

But the memories of that dancing class are not all tragic in atmosphere. There was the afternoon that I won the Elimination Prize with, as partner, a boy named Sidney Shurtleff (who is now a landscape architect and has changed *his* name to Shurcliff). The Elimination Contest was a part of the cotillion that marked the last dancing class of the season. Favors were given out, to be handed, grudgingly, to the girls by the boys; I think the last figure in the cotillion was the Elimination Contest. In principle, it was like musical chairs. Each couple was given a number, and we all danced — the fox trot, the one-step, the slide polka — and then abruptly the music would cease, and Miss Macomber would call out a few numbers drawn from a hat and the couples holding those numbers sat down. The last couple left dancing won. Sidney and I were the last couple left dancing, and side by side we marched the length of the small ballroom to receive our prizes. I do not remember what the prizes were. I remember the tune the lady at the piano was playing as we danced all alone the full circuit of the ballroom, as victors — a tune from the first World War called "Babes in the Wood." That last clumsily danced circuit — for we had not won our prize because of any talent, any superiority whatsoever, only by chance — was the high point of my life up to then. I tasted triumph.

The next set of memories I bear of the Copley Plaza is very different from these in mood. I must have been fourteen. I had begun going to Miss Winsor's School, out in Longwood, and I found it hard to make friends; as far as I could figure at that age, my total inability to play basketball or field hockey was the cause of my unpopularity. Some sort of instinct, right or wrong, caused me to begin stopping in at the Copley Plaza on my way home from school, in search of a kind of comfort, in search of a kind of distraction.

For here I would sit, in the main lobby, opposite to the huge marble desk, dressed in my thick, untidy school clothes, my galoshes, with my plaid schoolbag huddled into the thronelike chair with me, and watch what seemed to me the worldly and wealthy conducting their fascinating lives at the Copley Plaza. In from the Dartmouth Street entrance would hurry a bellboy, or two bellboys, laden down with expensive luggage, followed by a blond woman in a fur coat, or a close-shaven man in a check waistcoat, or a dark, romantic-looking lady all in black and attended by what seemed to be a governess with two or three rich, well-dressed children — important children, children with lives.

Occasionally I would get up and go down the corridor to the ladies' room, not so much because I needed to as that there I found myself not two feet away from beautiful, expensively dressed women who talked to each other busily about their approaching engagements. I would wash my hands, taking a long time about it, and listen to some lovely girl saying, "We're going to Paris Friday, on the *Ile*. . . ." Then I would go back to my throne in the lobby to watch some more people make their entrances. All the time, the stringed orchestra would be playing waltzes, behind in the palm court — fast and sweet and queerly nostalgic. It was almost as if this were the only life I had.

The final stage of my relationship with the Copley Plaza takes up where "Babes in the Wood" left off — on a note of triumph. I am a Boston debutante — a *popular* Boston debutante — going to those larger balls which are held here, and which, compared with the

dances at the Somerset, somehow never seem quite quite.
The Somerset is definitely quite quite. But now I go to
all those dances, too. My triumph is almost complete; I
have not had to *do* anything to achieve it, it just came,
as I grew older and had my hair shingled and began
being told I danced well and that I looked like Greta
Garbo. I feel a little superior toward balls at the Copley
Plaza.

Back in the old dressing room again. Now it is
thronged with girls: girls in knee-length evening dresses,
girls with rigid gold slave necklaces around their slender,
immature throats, girls in silver kid slippers and ostrich
leis and Chanel bracelets and pearls — pearls twisted
once close around the neck and left swinging down almost to the waist. The most beautiful girl of our year is
in black velvet, with a flesh chiffon bosom; she gazes as
though sightlessly into the big mirror as she applies eye
shadow to those fabulous eyelids. Someone says, "I hear
you made the Vincent. Congrats."

Mixed through the crowd, as though for their own
protection, are the pills — the girls with glasses, the girls
in pink taffeta dresses, the girls who played field hockey
so terribly well at Miss Winsor's. Later in the evening
they will retire here to the dressing room after a few too
many circlings of the ballroom in the same man's arms,
to wait alone until they summon courage to issue forth
once more. And here, like birds of a feather, chattering
together of Sherry's and the Meadowbrook, are the New

York girls — a little taller than anyone else, more glamorous, more unattainable, because they come from New York. They all the make the same joke — "The best thing about Beantown is the Merchants Limited going home." New York! It is the as yet unconquered, the next world.

We drift out, *dégagé*, a little blasé, to find the Harvard men with whom we came. Tails, they wore in those days. The small ballroom and the big ballroom are thrown open together to me now, and Billy Lossez's orchestra is playing. He has a banjo man who is supposed to be hot stuff and who has written a song, called "Afraid of You," that is rumored to have been inspired by one of the debutantes. *Which?* But the great Lossez specialty is "Je Ne Sais Pas Quoi Faire," delicate, a little melancholy; you sing it, in your best low, hoarse voice, into your partner's ear in the moment before the next man cuts in. "Do you belong to the Spee or the A.D.?" "Isn't Hope divine?" "How about coming tea dancing with me here tomorrow?" Tea dancing at the Copley Plaza — that was another facet of this coming-out diamond. But tonight is a ball, given by one of the hunting people out at Myopia for their lumpy daughter. The great thing is to be able to dance in a corner, with your own private stag line. The New York boys are the best dancers — they are snaky. But you are nice to everybody; it pays.

This is a really smooth dance; they are serving supper

throughout, with champagne continuously. We debutantes are only allowed to drink champagne. But some of the boys carry hip flasks, and the girls who are wild accept a sip from the flask when they go to sit out. That is another category of girl — the girls who go the limit. There are only a few of them and they are mentioned with bated breath.

I have met a new man. He is tall and rather an awkward dancer, but I know all about him; he is a big man in the Porcellian. After cutting back several times, he asks me if I would like to sit out, and I am delighted to.

We go to one of the small writing rooms; the girls with their beaux wander in and out. "Hello, Sarah." "Uh, hello." "Hello, Lily, Joe."

The hour is timeless. Outside, the Back Bay is fast asleep. Down the street, Childs is drowsing; we will go there for pancakes later. Only here is life going on, to the tune of "Je Ne Sais Pas Quoi Faire." "Darling, are you coming to my dance the twelfth?" "I wouldn't miss it." There are three dances on the twelfth — at the Somerset, here, and at the Women's Republican Club.

My new beau says, "Have you ever seen a loof?"

I say, "Never actually, but I've always imagined what one must look like."

"There must be hundreds of them," he says. "So many people seem to be aloof."

At one of the writing desks, we take turns, there in the sitting-out room at half past two in the morning, at drawing a loof. It has three eyes, a pointed head; its tongue sticks out permanently.

"Aren't you ever going to come back on the floor?" some man passing asks me, but I say, "I'm busy drawing a loof." "A *what?*" We laugh, and here my memories fade away, and end.

It is these memories that make the Copley Plaza seem to me like a showy, faintly second-rate, meretricious mother that nonetheless did give me a kind of life. You can't make my mother into somebody different by suddenly beginning to call her Mrs. Sheraton.

But, if I know the Bostonians, they will keep right on calling the old hotel the Copley Plaza anyway.

15

By CHILDREN, A SECRET CAN STILL BE SENSUOUSLY
appreciated as if it were a ripe plum bitten into — or,
rather, like the surprise a chocolate peppermint, allowed
to dissolve upon the tongue, gradually divulges. For the
secret that involves a receptacle is the secret of secrets, as
children recognize. Thus, when Jinny Welch — the one
of the Welch children across the street nearest to my
age, and my best friend — and I discovered a secret
drawer in the mahogany highboy in our dining room,
we gave each other one intense look and within minutes
had founded a club about it.

First, to check up on the authenticity of our find, we
consulted my mother. She was making a charcoal drawing upstairs in her bedroom, seated before her easel in a
low chair beside the window, outside which snow was
slowly falling.

We had dashed up the narrow old staircase in our
excitement, but we slowed down on entering the room,
and edged in, our skirts switching. "I was just looking

for something, in the highboy," I began cautiously. I had never actually been forbidden the highboy, where table linen was kept, but on the other hand one never knew what would suddenly arouse sleeping prohibitions.

My mother looked away from her drawing, over the tops of her glasses. She appeared to be considering my remark. Dark-haired Jinny, ever more passionate and more trusting than I, was unable to persevere with such tactical maneuvers.

"Did you know that the sticking-out thing at the top of your highboy pulls out, and you can put things inside?" she demanded.

My mother smiled. "The molding," she defined it. "Yes. That's the secret drawer. Your grandfather used to keep securities in it," she added to me. "Just don't pull the whole piece of furniture down on top of yourselves."

But we were out of the room. A secret drawer! And from her placid tone she might have been speaking of fish balls.

We knew just what our next step must be. Jinny would be president, I would be secretary and treasurer. It would be called the Secret Drawer Club, and we would keep May, Jinny's younger sister, out. The boys, Tom and Royal Welch, would hear only enough of it from us to know they were being kept out, too. As for the secret drawer itself, we would use it to hide things in. The bylaws, for one thing, could be hidden in it, once we had them drawn up.

We sat right down at the round dining-room table to start work on them, with a pad of lined school paper, and some pencils, from my father's study, that smelled of cedar. A pale white light came in through the windows as, outside, snow continued to fall. "1. The members of the Secret Drawer Club must be honorable," I wrote, and licked the delicious graphite. "2. The members of the Secret Drawer Club must have grit. 3. The Secretary and Treasurer is not allowed to open the Secret Drawer unless the President is present. 4. . . ."

Almost as beavers are led to build dams, at the occurrence of any striking or unusual event we tended to form a club about it. Sometimes it was one of us who was left out of a new organization, sometimes another, but it was part of the very soul of club-forming to leave somebody out. Once I even had a club with Tom and Royal against the girls. That club had something to do with a pine tree we had found, far back in the woods, whose branches hung low to the ground and made a dark shelter. It was called the Pine Tree Club and its bylaws began, "All girls except the Corresponding Secretary are forbidden to get within ten (10) feet of the Sacred Pine Tree."

The bylaws of our clubs invariably had a high moral tone, and were strong on the stoical virtues as requirements for membership — loyalty, courage, silence under torture. Mr. Thompson Welch once in a while got wind of one of our clubs and forced it out into the open. "The children must be made to go through with their projects" was his favorite maxim. At such words my parents, who wanted only to be left in peace to paint, would groan, when they thought I was not around.

The Legion of Honor was one of the clubs that Mr. Welch exploited. Originally called the Pantry Club, it had had a membership composed of May, Royal, Tom, and me, Jinny being the one it was against. It had met to suck lemons and eat cookies, raisins, and whatever other provender offered, in the Welches' pantry on Thursday afternoons, when their cook and waitress were off. Its bylaws expressed the usual high-minded ideals, of which May — the youngest Welch child and the only one toward whom Mr. Welch made an occasional demonstration of affection — unfortunately let drop some details while sitting on that sharkskin knee.

May was, at that age, a naturally cuddly child, fond of kissing, and furthermore she was fundamentally rather stupid. Poor May was never to learn to distrust the keen, close-shaven face pressed against her plump one in the way that the other Welch children did, at the same time that they maintained an absolutely sincere filial awe and regard. Proud declarations of "Father says" and "Father believes" were mingled, by them, with rigid caution about ever telling Father anything, in a combination only beset children could achieve.

That was how the Pantry Club came to turn into the

Legion of Honor — an organization dedicated to character improvement, with tattletale features built in, and a membership which, of course, had been enlarged to include Jinny. Its officers were Mr. Welch, as General, and, with great reluctance, my parents, as Colonel and Major. On meeting one of these superiors, a Legionnaire was supposed to salute and, if required, to recite the by-laws, now called regulations, which had once been those of the Pantry Club. "I will put honor above all. I will be upright in everything. I will be pure in word and deed. . . ." Naturally, this institution soon died on the vine, as it lacked at least two of the essential ingredients of a satisfactory society — secrecy and exclusiveness.

Once in a while I, an only child, would make some important discovery, and then I faced the tremendous choice between sharing it and possessing a secret all alone. A secret secret is not the same as a shared secret. It belongs to the order of loneliness, not to the order of societies. But loneliness is not to be despised. Its private joys are especially burning. The day I found a fortune in bills, hidden away in a secret hiding place in the dining room, seemed to set me apart from the Welches in a way both painful and exalting.

Our dining room was always a place for discoveries and surprises, if only of new sights and the sensations that went with them, such as the after-dinner coffee cups on the top shelf of the china cabinet. I had climbed on a dining-room chair to see what I could see, and what

I saw was those tiny cups — round-bowled, thin as egg-shells, painted with bouquets of imperishably lovely flowers, with grass-green rims and handles. Another time it was a plate, at the bottom of a pile of ordinary white Wedgwood plates that I had lifted out of the cupboard, having spied a scalloped rim that did not match. What but the pink-and-white face of Louis XIV, of all people, should be gazing up at me off that plate from under his curly full wig!

I found the money in an old-fashioned card table with a lyre-shaped base, which was used as a serving table. My parents referred to it as the Duncan Phyfe, though with an air of doubt. Fiddling with its top, I felt the top slide. I pulled the table a little out from the wall and slid the top farther around — it moved as though on a pivot — and there, underneath, in a shallow flat space, lay the green bills. I counted them. There were four. They were mine. I was rich. Worlds spun, and exploded in showers of gold.

"Look what I found!" I announced to my mother, who was passing through the dining room at that moment, wearing the distracted expression she assumed when domestic duty called and she wanted to get back to painting.

"The money for the china horse!" she exclaimed, and reached out her hand. "I knew I'd put it somewhere. Was it in the card table?"

I stared at her.

"I *found* it," I said.

My mother appeared to recollect something of juvenile mores. She withdrew her outstretched hand and sighed. "I don't know when I shall be able to get that horse," she complained. "It's still at Carbone's, but I don't know how much longer it will stay there." She departed on her hurried errand, and I was left alone with the pelf, feeling powerful, Midan, and guilty. I would not share my secret with the Welches, I knew, for then I would have to share what I had discovered, too.

What we discovered one rainy spring afternoon in the Welches' attic was far more than an ordinary secret and at the same time something less than one. Mr. Welch, of course, had to know about it, and at once began telling his fashionable friends, as he took them on tours of the old house. And yet, for all its airing, what we discovered always retained for us the quality of a secret, something that could be tasted in private, forever, upon the tongue of imagination.

The Welches' was an ancient New England house, with a gambrel roof, that had been a tavern in colonial times. It had no third story; the attic was an unfinished space under the eaves on the second floor, reached from one of the bedrooms by a small, low, crooked door. We used to play in there — as we were doing on that particular afternoon — when we couldn't go out; it was a useful place for getting away from the cheery rallying of Miss Perkins, the English governess. She did not like to stoop to go through the crooked door, or risk her hair net against the rough beams festooned with cobwebs.

Dingy light came sifting in through a small, square window at each gable end of the slant-roofed, long, narrow room. Jinny and May were playing checkers on the floor under one of the windows. I was drawing a castle with four turrets that pierced through some clouds and came out at the top again. Tom, who had a very precise mind, was standing beside the checkerboard, criticizing his sisters' play. "You can take three of her men," he observed as May's plump hand hovered above the board. "Can't you see it? No, naturally I'm not going to tell you."

Royal had that morning found, lying on the table beside Tom's bed, a copy of a book called *Youth Faces Life*. Now he had it propped within the coils of his long, leggy frame, down at the other end of the attic, by the window. Who had put the book by Tom's bed? Tom did not know. That was the way improving information often was introduced into the Welch household — a pamphlet entitled *The Christian Faith* would appear by Jinny's place at dinner, a book called *Jolly Tennis Days* on the bedside table of May, who hated physical exertion. It gave a faintly eerie quality to their education, always to be coming upon these anonymously placed guides to perfection.

" 'A cold shower and brisk exercise will be found to

prove the soundest medicine for the youthful mind that strays to wasteful daydreams,' " Royal read aloud, snorting.

"Shut up, Royal," Tom said, uneasily. Royal was and always had been unpredictable, unreliable, and dangerous. His were ever the severest of the penances given out — the whole lawn to mow, the whole hedge to clip, two hours of Latin a morning — at those week-end assemblies when Mr. Welch dealt out, with a cold, legal hand, retribution for the week's errors.

" 'The author views coeducational systems with some misgiving,' " Royal continued. " 'Propinquity often gives rise to daydreams far in advance of the youth's emotional development, which in turn can lead —' "

"Shut up!" Tom said, louder. He went down to the other end of the attic and attempted to wrench the book away from Royal. They began to wrestle over it — monkey-faced, curly-haired Royal and his handsome older brother.

We girls were elaborately not paying any attention. Then the struggle had suddenly ceased and Royal was kneeling, peering down into a gap in the boarding of the benchlike structure around the huge chimney that rose through the middle of the attic. "The boards just moved when I hit against them," he said, in a strangled voice. "It goes way down inside. I can't see how far."

May ran for her Christmas flashlight. All of us elbowed one another to get a view. Flashlight in hand, Royal prepared to let himself down into the hole, but Tom took the flashlight away from him. "I will go first," he announced, in tones of the eldest, "and see if it's safe."

It *was* safe. It was a secret passage, a real one, built on purpose at some unknown time for some unknown purpose. Hiding from Indians? Concealing fugitive slaves? You let yourself down into the hole by the chimney until your feet struck bottom. Then, crouched double, you went along a narrow walkway around the chimney to the opposite side of it, where a flight of steps went down to the entrance to a room, perhaps six feet long, four feet wide, and five feet high, built all of brick within that wooden house. You were, by that time, on a level with the ground-floor rooms. The brick chamber had a narrow shelf that ran along one end. On it we found lying some rusty nails.

Through an opening between the last beam and the chimney, beside the entrance to the brick room, you could let yourself down the rough stone wall of the cellar. Looking up from there, no one would ever have suspected that where the stone wall met the heavy beams supporting the ground floor was a gap that a slim man could get through.

That slim man Mr. Welch did get through it once, from above, to test the veracity of our breathless claims of having discovered a secret passage. Arrived at the cellar, he brushed off the creases of his trousers and the shoulders of his well-tailored suit. Then, slapping his hands briskly together, he remarked, "I must tell old Appleton of this. Old Corky Appleton, president of the Massachusetts Historical Society. And, I understand," he added reflectively, "of the Somerset Club as well."

But even after having heard our secret passage described to expensively scented ladies in summer furs as they paused gracefully at the top of the stairs; even after the house had become, on Mr. Welch's tongue, "my little gem of a seventeenth-century house in the country with, you know, a secret passage whose authenticity my good friend Corky Appleton personally vouches for" — even then, the secret passage remained, for us, a secret. In fact, I think that in some mysterious way it was a secret secret to each of us.

Twenty years later, when May lay dying in that slum where Jinny had finally discovered her, too late for her alcoholism to be treated, the young doctor we had got hold of came out of the bedroom into the dirty parlor where we waited, and said, "You can go in now. She's delirious. She keeps talking about a passage with somebody dead stuck in it. Mean anything to you?"

As we went into the bedroom, we gave each other a searching look, and Jinny said slowly, "Do you know, when I was carrying the children, I always imagined them as being curled up inside the brick room."

As for me, it was the Welches' house that I always saw in my mind's eye when I imagined growing up and going out into the world. It was as if that house across the street *were* getting away from home. And when I was out in the world, I imagined, I would be secure within the secret passage — in the core, the hidden heart, of that house.

The summer after we discovered the secret passage, we used to play prisoners'-base and tag, as we had every summer, with the Harrington children from down the road. In the long dusks after supper, when the light was slowly failing across the poison-green grass of the Welches' lawn, our voices calling out "Not It!" sounded mysterious and far away. We used to play hide-and-go-seek, and a game called sardines-in-a-box. In this game only one player hid, and the others went separately to find him. Each player who found him would join him and keep still, until in the end one lone player would be wandering the twilight grounds in desperation, convinced that there had been from the start a conspiracy against him. The secret passage was the favorite for a sardine box — so favorite that it became too easy, once the Harrington children learned of it, and then good again because everybody supposed everybody else was avoiding it, too.

I was the sardine, one evening, and I slipped down the hole in the attic and around the passage we all now knew so well that we needed no flashlight. In the pitch-darkness of the brick room I crouched, and willed Tom Welch to be the first one to join me.

The kind of wasteful daydreaming referred to by the author of *Youth Faces Life* had been running riot in me all summer. In my bedroom at home there was a brownish-tinged print of Sir Galahad, standing beside his charger, that was, it seemed to me, a perfect portrait of Tom — smooth-haired, gallant-faced, and noble. All those exalted ideals that we had expressed in the bylaws of our innumerable clubs seemed all at once to have found their realization in him.

Now I set my mind to the telepathic technique I had been working on lately, which had already yielded up a gold bangle, my first piece of jewelry. I had willed my parents to give it to me for my June birthday. *Come,* I thought confidently, visualizing Tom. I could feel the knot of concentration forming between my eyes that was an essential part of the technique. *Come to the secret passage.*

Soon I heard footsteps moving softly around the chimney. I held my breath. Someone crouched down beside me in that narrow space, an arm was put around me, and little, wet kisses were pressed upon my face.

I was terribly shocked. Those wet lips felt disgusting. But, as usual when I shrank from something, I had an instant reflex to conceal my revulsion. As usual, I feared I was naïve. If this was what kissing was like, I told my fainting mind, it must be nice, because Tom was doing it. Trying to co-operate, I put my hand up behind his head as he kissed me.

The hair I touched was rough and curly. It was not Tom at all; it was Royal.

But I let the odious little kisses continue, because I felt in some obscure way that if I pushed him off, it would give away who I had imagined was kissing me. Tom was my secret secret. And a secret secret is against everybody — sometimes even against oneself.

16

Nowadays when i make a trip to washington it is to go to the dentist. It takes two and a half hours by train from Charlottesville, where I live, and I am apt to wear a tailored suit and carry a coat, in case it turns colder, and an umbrella, in case it rains. After the dentist has finished with me I replace my lipstick and, since I was brought up to expect an ice-cream soda after the dentist, I generally go to see my friend Miss Dorothy Armistead, who lives in a fusty old apartment near Thomas Circle and dresses in genuine antiques. (Since she would be enraged if her privacy was invaded, the name I use is not a real one, and neither are most of the names in this book.) Sometimes I merely pay a call and am given kitchen tea out of a Royal Worcester pot that belonged to one of Miss Dorothy's ancestors at Beaulieu, in Virginia; sometimes we go to the National Gallery or to a concert.

Miss Dorothy's exalted lineage and her moral stand-ards, which are Victorian, permit her to view Washington society with a very cold eye indeed. It is both entertaining and salutary to observe our nation's capital through the dun-colored glasses of her lorgnette, in which most people of means become *nouveaux riches;* distinguished diplomats, as foreigners, appear fundamentally shabby; and Georgetown, that community of the fashionable rich, is a sort of slum. "A very damp, unsanitary place," Miss Dorothy calls it.

Last time I had to go to the dentist Miss Dorothy and I went to a piano recital. We heard Mozart at the beginning of the program, but I don't know what came after that, for after the first number Miss Dorothy — who classes musicians, along with actors, as mummers and unfit for consideration or Christian burial — whispered sibilantly to me, "See that woman — with the ragged stuff on her hat? That's Diana de Carville. I suppose you've heard of her?" She gave the name the vanishing *y* of old Virginia, so that it sounded like "Cyarville."

I nodded vigorously as the pianist again lifted his hands to the keys. I had indeed heard of her. I was almost unconscious of the music as I continued to stare at the profile of the handsome woman with the black monkey-fur cap over her silver hair, several rows ahead of us. I had never before actually seen the face that in my youth was a legend in the cities up and down the Eastern seaboard, but twenty-five years ago I had been eaten up with jealousy of its owner.

I will never know the reasons — cultural? patriotic? — that made my mother take me out of my Boston school for a week, when I was fifteen, and allow me to accompany her to Washington, where she was to serve on the jury of selection at the Corcoran Gallery of Art. I was not to stay with her at the hotel where the jurists were being put up but with my cousin Lelia, in the house on N Street where our paternal grandfather had lived when he was Chaplain of the Senate in Teddy Roosevelt's administration. The house was now owned by his oldest son, who was very unlike my artist father, being the social member of the family; he had been heard to remark that in his travels for the Pennsylvania Railroad he liked to be able to put up at his own club no matter what city he found himself in.

Lelia, though only a little older than I, was making her debut in Washington. "Advanced for her age" was the family slug for Lelia. Perhaps my parents thought it would be nice for me, an only child, to see something, under conditions of girlish festivity, of a female relative of similar years; I don't know. In any case I doubt whether my parents, who, contrary to the popular conception of artists, were innocent and unworldly in the extreme, realized what my visit would be like.

Lelia met me at the door when I arrived, after dark. I turned and waved reassuringly at my mother, leaning out of a waiting taxi. She waved back and the taxi drove on.

166

"Well. It's been aeons since we've met," Lelia drawled as we went into the lighted hall.

She was tall, blond, and dressed in a black crepe-de-Chine dress, with oblong, braid-edged, overlapping flaps down the skirt, that even my Boston eye recognized as being French; I was later instructed that it came from Patou's. She wore lipstick. She wore earrings. I nearly died right there in the hall.

After I had spoken to my uncle and aunt, Lelia showed me up to my room, on the fourth floor, where I unpacked my garments from Jordan Marsh's and R. H. Stearns — serviceable wool dresses for daytime, a brown velveteen "suitable if they should take you to a tea," my taffeta evening dress, of a clear and guileless pink, with, at the hip, a tinsel rose that had looked dashing back in Boston.

As I hung them in the closet Lelia sat gazing at her image in the mirror of my dressing table. She picked up the hand mirror and squinted intently at the skin on her nose. Then she held the mirror farther away from her face. "God, how beautiful I am tonight," she said.

It has occurred to me in later years that Lelia, "advanced for her age," perhaps meant to be funny. At the time all I felt was awe and thorough agreement.

"We're going to a supper dance this evening," she said, laying the mirror down and turning around. "Two divine creatures are coming here to dinner first."

At this use of the word "divine" my brain reeled.

"I do hope your family lets you drink," Lelia continued. "We'll all have cocktails at eight, of course, in the Chinese Room. Your creature is named Morgan Hughes. He's in the diplomatic. He's been literally shattered in love and I don't suppose he will ever entirely recover. Diana de Carville, of course. I thought you might soothe him."

As my organism struggled to adjust itself to this responsibility, Lelia went on. "My creature is Russian. White. He's suffered horribly, of course."

The phrase "of course" has never again sounded to me quite the way it did on that trip to Washington: world-weary, nostalgic, saturated with sophistication. What I felt mostly was gratitude at being tacitly included. "Of course," I agreed, to I knew not what.

The Chinese Room at eight turned out to be my grandfather's old study, which, true enough, had always had a pair of orange-and-gold Chinese vases on top of one of the bookcases; Lelia had added some Chinese carved-stone ash trays and a cigarette box to match. But to me, totally englamoured and always a pushover for nomenclature, it might as well have been the Dowager Empress's palace at Peking.

The two young men arrived in white tie and tails. Lelia had on a white-and-silver sheath, in which she looked taller and slimmer and blonder than ever. I, perforce, wore pink taffeta.

"Make the Orange Blossoms, will you, Morgan?" Lelia commanded with a weary air. "Don't forget to put in a little Five Fruit." Then, turning to the other man, she burst into fluent French; Lelia had gone to school in Switzerland. The Russian, introduced to me as Serge Sokolov, replied and then, turning to me, said something that ended in *"n'est-ce pas, mademoiselle?"*

For all eleven school years of my life I had studied French, but those were the only words I understood. *"Je ne comprends pas,"* I said miserably, with a Boston accent. Were they going to talk only French?

To my rescue came my divine creature, who seemed indeed divine, being well over six feet tall, dark, with eyebrows that met, deliriously, in the middle.

"One gets tired of the incessant babble of foreign languages in Washington," he observed wearily, handing me a glass. "English is so much more chic, of course."

I smiled at him gratefully and began on my life's first cocktail. More than anything else it reminded me of castor oil, which I had always been given to take mixed with orange juice.

The supper dance was, I think, at the Carlton. The ballroom looked beautiful. Chandeliers of cut crystal blazed; long glass French doors stood open on a terrace where romantic-looking couples strayed away from the floor; there were glimpses of foreign uniforms, rows of medals and gold braid, as their dashing wearers swooped in and out of the dance with Washington beauties in their arms. The robes-de-style that were just beginning to be worn in those days swung wide in sweeps of pale, lovely colors — mauve, silver gray, and dusty rose. Waiters glided around the edges of the room passing great trays of champagne in bell-shaped glasses.

As for me, after a short turn with Morgan Hughes I danced round and round and round, in my pink taffeta dress, with Mr. Sokolov.

It was a nightmare — all heaven outside me and all hell within. I had said everything I could think of to say, about how good the floor was and how pretty the girls were and wasn't it warm for November? I felt so sorry for Mr. Sokolov that my heart ached. Was he, then, always to suffer? As my heart was going down for the third time, my partner suddenly leaped away from me like a released spring. Morgan Hughes had cut in. I looked up at those eyebrows. He had rescued me again.

"Would you care to go out on the terrace?" he asked after one circuit of the floor. "I feel like talking."

"Of course," I said. They were the only words I knew that sounded right, any more.

We passed through the French doors and out into the damp, cool air. Morgan leaned against the parapet and lighted a cigarette.

And that was the first time I heard about Diana de Carville, although already, while still in her teens, she was a legend — one of those occasional young girls in the Eastern cities who became famous even before they made their debuts. Rumors had leaked out from the very schoolroom, via awe-struck guests at her Texas mother's Massachusetts Avenue dinner parties, of her great beauty, her multilingual virtuosity, her extraordinary charm. She seemed marked out from birth for personal celebrity.

Her childhood had been fantastic — a much-publicized succession of kidnapings by her French viscount father, litigations, reinstatements at her mother's establishments in Washington and Bar Harbor. It had been enough to ruin the life of most children, but Diana had emerged from it with a creamy serenity that made her admirers swoon.

"Her eyes are purple," Morgan Hughes insisted to me, feverishly, as he lit his seventh or eighth cigarette. He must have been finding me the perfect listener. Between the glamour of Diana de Carville and his own divinity, I could only gaze in silence, with all the attentive sympathy any lover could ask. "Her hair is the color of nasturtiums," he said. "Of course, the Italians go mad."

"Of course," I said.

By the time we went back into the ballroom I was hopelessly in love myself. It was the first time I had experienced the tender passion, unless you count the little boy named Charlie in my kindergarten, whom I once kissed because he had such beautiful round pink cheeks.

I had been, I realize now, swept up in what is surely the most insidious web in the world — hearing an attractive man tell how he feels about his beloved. Any girl will identify herself with the adored one, and thus become the recipient of a love distilled into perfection through being at one remove. Many an experienced charmer has been carried off her feet in this way, and I was no charmer and anything but experienced. On the way back to N Street that night, Washington seemed to be a city of total magic, with its white marble mansions, its stately circles each with a fountain or a statue, its majestic avenues, all seen by the white twinkling lights of one in the morning. Probably nobody has ever appreciated M. L'Enfant's handiwork more thoroughly than I did.

With the humility of childhood, I never expected to see Morgan Hughes again. I was reconciled to the prospect of spending the remainder of my life in love with a memory. To tell the truth, tragic and unrequited as I knew my passion to be, I was enjoying it very much. Lelia, it turned out, had rather a crush on Sokolov, who sent her boxes of loose gardenias that arrived at the breakfast table, to my uncle's great disapproval; he would give a sniff and peer over the top of his Washington *Post* at the green waxed paper foaming out of the florist's box, as if to say, "Flowers? At breakfast?" But Sokolov's calls had not been discouraged, and he used to play to us, on the piano in the Chinese Room, the tune of his Czarist regimental marching song. After he had gone, Lelia would play it over with one finger, and I would sit on the sofa thinking of Morgan. The tune, at once gay and heartbreaking, gallant and doomed, seemed exactly to fit my mood.

"Serge has nothing left to live for," Lelia would say as she turned from the piano. "Can you think of anything more divine?"

That week, we went to lunch at Rauscher's, then the fashionable Washington restaurant, and once, with my uncle, at the Cosmos Club on Lafayette Square, which, since it had a view from its front door of the White House, may have come under the heading of educational. We went to teas, where I wore my suitable brown velveteen and noticed how my aunt and the other ladies left cards in a silver urn near the door. We went to a dinner at Chevy Chase, and to a dance at the Hungarian Legation, where a *Zigeuner* orchestra played waltz music with fast, reckless longing — the pretty, precocious Lelia and her lump of a cousin from Boston.

The morning before the day I was to leave, the telephone rang and Lelia answered it. I saw her glance at me with a peculiar expression.

"I'm sure she'd adore it," she said. She turned away from the instrument to me. "You *would* like to go to tea with Morgan this afternoon, wouldn't you?" she asked.

I swallowed hard and nodded.

"She would," Lelia reported to the soul of my soul. Thus was made my first date.

He called for me in N Street that afternoon at four, an irresistibly sophisticated figure in a coonskin coat. We drove by taxi to the Willard, in those days called the New Willard, where marble-floored courts with potted palms awaited us and where we were led by an obsequious headwaiter to a white-covered table for two. Morgan ordered tea and cinnamon toast. I remember it was the first time I had ever tasted cinnamon toast. But I was having trouble breathing. Satan had entered the Eden of my childhood state and introduced the fancy that Morgan had fallen prey to just such a passion for me as I entertained for him. "I have never encountered such sympathy and understanding," he would begin pretty soon. "I cannot let you go away without . . ." Even the Devil himself could not conjecture how that sentence would end.

But the sentence never started. Morgan just wanted to talk some more about Diana de Carville, who since I saw him last had granted him something called a late date, only to break it again. He had found me sympathetic and understanding, all right.

As the orchestra behind the palms went on playing hotel music — "Les Patineurs," I remember, and "Roses of the South" — as beautiful women in rich furs strolled past us accompanied by handsome ambassadorial types, and I sipped the tea into which I had dropped a consoling five lumps of sugar, my vain fancy became converted into its concomitant of envy of Diana de Carville. Oh, to live in Washington and speak five languages! To have purple eyes and a marble mansion and a Roman admirer who had tried to drown himself for one, to be beautiful and fascinating and hard of heart, to be able to make men suffer!

Morgan took me home in another taxicab. I shall never forget the way he looked as he took me up to the door of the N Street house, his dark head bare, his coon coat flapping below his knees.

"Good-by," he said. "Let me know when you come back to Washington. You're going to turn out divine."

Not quite fainting, I entered the house. In the room on the left of the hall my uncle was laying out bridge problems. "Have you enjoyed yourself?" he inquired.

Next morning I took the Colonial home to Boston. My mother had gone two or three days before, at the close of the jury's deliberations; it had been thought suitable that I be allowed to travel alone. My uncle accompanied me to the Union Station and walked down the long, long platform with me to my Pullman car. As we passed the waiting Pennsylvania Railroad conductors and brakemen and the Pullman porters, they tipped their caps and said, "Good morning, Mr. Hale." When we reached my car, my uncle took out two whole dollars and handed them to the beaming colored attendant standing by the steps. "Take care of this little girl, George," he said.

I was so impressed that it almost made up to me for not being recognized as the woman who had suffered that I was.

I never did let Morgan Hughes know when I came back to Washington again, for by that time I was in the process of making my own debut — or, as we called it in Boston, coming out — and had been invited to Washington to go to the debutante parties there in the holidays. One afternoon when an ardent West Pointer took me to tea at the Willard, I did remember that other, first tea date, but with the pitying emotion that one used for looking back on childhood.

I always kept a little stab of special envy for Diana de Carville, however. Over the years, in dentists' waiting rooms and under the dryer at the hairdresser's, I followed her career in the pages of the fashion magazines. Against a background of the buzzing of the drill or the roaring of the dryer I would scan with intensity those pictures of her infallibly beautiful face.

Although I never met her — she had been skiing at Sestrières that winter I came out and went to Washington — I also never felt that she was just someone I had seen pictures of. I was connected to her by emotional bonds; she meant something painful and desirable to me.

And so, at that Washington concert to which I had gone with Miss Dorothy Armistead, it was with the liveliest curiosity that — dressed in my tailored suit, my umbrella planted safely between my knees, my feet too hot from wearing rubbers — I continued to gaze at the legendary profile a few rows ahead of me.

When the intermission came, I turned to my companion and said, "Isn't she wonderful?"

Miss Dorothy raised her battered lorgnette and took a good stare at Diana de Carville, who was coming up the aisle from her seat, chattering to a friend: tall, beautiful, exotic, and haggard.

"Who, her?" Miss Dorothy said. "Common as pig tracks."

"Oh, Miss Dorothy, come on, now!" I protested. "She's had the most glamorous life of anybody in my generation."

Miss Dorothy considered the glamorous life of Diana de Carville.

"Cheap doings," she summed it up.

"But she was married to a prince," I said feebly.

"He was common as pig tracks, too," Miss Dorothy said. Briskly she put her lorgnette away in a preposterous bead bag that had belonged to some extinct Armistead of Beaulieu. "Let us go outside and take the air," she proposed.

17

I NEVER WENT TO A BOARDING SCHOOL. I WENT TO DAY school in Boston, and I never liked it, but I think I would have hated boarding school more, because I would have had to work, and I never did any work in school after I stopped being a child and started being interested in boys. The girls I knew started being interested in boys when we were about fifteen, and the years that we were sixteen and seventeen most of us were allowed to have boys call on us in the evenings after supper.

When we were fifteen, we used to talk about boys, but once our families started letting us have callers, we never talked about them much any more and stopped bragging about how many boys we knew. All of us knew, though, which girls were popular and which ones were allowed to go driving with boys and all about each other. We never talked about what boys called on us the evening before, but we used to write the names of the boys we liked on the sides of our schoolbooks when we were not paying attention in class, printing the names or the

178

initials against the grain of the closed edges of the pages.

Sometimes boys used to call for us at school, around four in the afternoon, at the end of afternoon sports. The school didn't like it, but they couldn't stop it. The cloakroom was down in the basement of the building, and we used to look out of the windows that were flush with the ground and see what boys were waiting out on the driveway. They used to stay in their cars so that the girls coming out the door wouldn't stare at them, but when the girl a boy was waiting for came out, he would have to come over to the entrance to meet her, because no girl would cross over and get into a boy's car with him sitting there.

It was funny how little we used to care what boy we were with. I don't think it made any difference to us then; we were just interested and excited in finding out whether we were going to be popular with boys or not. I don't remember anything about what boys I saw when I was sixteen; I just remember a lot of brown tweed coats and a red Nash Six roadster I used to go driving in, and I remember that the boys I used to see then thought it was awful to put anything on their hair.

When I was seventeen, I never did much homework at night. When boys came to call, you would hear the chains on their cars grinding on the frozen snow out on the road as they turned around in the driveway. Then they would come in and sit in front of the fire in the living room, and my father would talk to them as long as he could stand it, and then he would go into his study and shut the door. The boys used to wear rubber-soled shoes which would smell after a while from being near the fire. The boys sat on the floor or on footstools and talked, and sometimes we would go to the movies.

The movies I was allowed to go to were in the next town to ours. They were upstairs in an old frame building, and you went up some dusty bare stairs and groped in the darkness for seats. They used to have Western serials, and after every picture they would flash on the advertisements, printed by hand in big, sprawling letters, of shops in the town. Lots of times the advertisement would be thrown on the screen upside down, and then the town boys in the audience would clap and stamp and whistle. At the end of all the movies they flashed on a picture of two babies sitting in a basket of roses and a sign saying GOOD NIGHT.

I don't remember anything about Dave Page before that night, sitting in the movies, when he reached in my lap and took my hand and held it. I don't know where I met him, I don't know who brought him out to my house, I don't remember who else went to the movies with us. But my hand had never been held by a boy before. I stopped seeing the movie. I let him hold my hand and tried to hold it still and relaxed. He let go of it once for a few minutes, and suddenly I was worried about it and I wondered if it was because he didn't like holding it, but then he took it again. It felt awkward and I couldn't relax my hand, but I didn't want him to stop. He didn't look at me at all, but I looked at him in the queer movie-house light and that is the first memory I have of seeing him. He had curly hair cut very short the way boys did, and a short nose and a mouth like a girl's and a round chin. I kept looking at him, and when the lights went on and we got up and went down the wooden stairs, I felt queer and excited and afraid to look at him at all.

There was always deep snow those winters that lasted all winter long. Dave Page took me to the movies often that winter, and he always held my hand and he always stopped holding it for a little while and I would worry about why he had stopped. There was always another boy with us, because my family would not allow me to go to the movies with just one boy, and we would drive home afterward in the cold, bright night along the rutted roads, three in the front seat. They would come in the house when we got home, and we would get the hot chocolate that was on the stove in the kitchen and the sandwiches on the dining-room table. After that first night when he held my hand in the movies, I used to think about Dave Page all the time and he was the only boy that I couldn't talk to.

After supper in the evenings, I often went up to my room and sat on the bed beside the window with the lights off to watch for cars coming to our house. I could tell Dave Page's car because it had four headlights, two big ones and two little ones above. The cars would go by on the road with the white lights bobbing jerkily over the bluish snow, and some nights one would turn at the corner and I could tell right away if it was Dave Page's.

Sometimes he came alone, and we sat down in the living room in front of the fire and I would try to talk to him, but all I could ever do was look at him. He was tall and his face was always burned dark red and he played hockey on his school team, but I couldn't talk to him about hockey or anything else. When he came, I took a long time before I went downstairs to see him, trying to think of things that I would talk to him about, but when I sat down and he sat down on the other side of the fire on the floor, I could not talk to him at all.

In the Easter vacation there was a holiday dance for the girls my age, and several boys asked me to go with them and I said I wouldn't, because I hoped Dave Page would ask me to go with him. But he never did, and in the end I went with someone else, I've forgotten who.

I remember the dance, though. It was in a hall in town, and a lot of the girls' mothers were patronesses and there was a woman who was running the dance and she wore a dress made of blue glass spangles. The music sounded very loud and wild in the big hall, and the stags stood in a big, shifting mass in the middle of the room. The girls who weren't having a good time sat along the wall on gilt chairs near the patronesses and pretended that they were waiting for someone. They kept looking eager, and they tapped with their feet and looked over toward the punch table as if they were impatient for someone who was bringing them something. The girls who were having a good time danced in the corners, and there were little separate groups of stags around them.

Almost all the boys I knew that year danced with me, but I kept looking over their shoulders to see if Dave Page had come. I could not think about the party or having a good time or anything except Dave Page. The backs of boys' heads would look like the back of his head, and then they would turn around and it would be someone else. When the music stopped and we walked over to the crowd around the punch table, and when a boy asked me to sit out in the chairs along the wall, I was always looking for Dave.

When I did see him, he was dancing with someone else and he didn't see me, and after that everything was a sort of fog and I didn't hear anything boys said until Dave Page cut in and I was dancing with him. I felt so strange about dancing with him — queer and light, and my hands were cold. I wanted to float in his arms, but I felt very awkward and my feet were heavy. I looked up at his dark-burned face and thought how wonderful it was to be dancing with him, and it didn't seem stupid not to have anything to say.

183

I remember how the music stopped and how sudden it was and how we stood in the middle of the big floor. When he let go of me, I felt as if I wasn't going to be able to stand up. We stood there, and you could hear all the people talking at once now the music had stopped, and the sound of their feet scuffling along the dance floor as they walked to the chairs or the punch table.

I remember he said, "I know a place where we can sit out outside."

I wanted to go anywhere he wanted to go. We went out of a small door that led to a fire escape and a flight of back stairs. There was nothing to sit on but a high stool that stood in the little hall, and I sat on it and he stood beside me and smoked a cigarette. I couldn't think of anything to say. Pretty soon I could hear the music beginning again inside. It sounded queer and echoing and very far away. Dave Page just stood beside me and I looked at the black cloth of his coat that was opposite my eyes. Then he threw his cigarette on the floor and stepped on it.

I looked up at him and he was looking at me. His eyes were bright blue. He looked straight at me and I looked at him, and then he kissed me.

I never felt like that any other time in my life. I felt warm inside my body suddenly, and high up in the sky and floating and so happy that it felt like a spire that tapered off far up in the stars. I felt all that in one second.

He kissed me once, and then he straightened up and I looked at him. His hair was black and his face was dark red and his eyes were blue. He smiled at me and held out his arm for me to take. I slid off the stool and took his arm and walked back into the dance hall without seeing where I was going.

Someone cut in on him right away, and then more people danced with me. Dave Page cut in on me several more times that night, and when he would cut in, all the fog that I was in would disappear and I would dance in his arms and feel terribly aware of him and wish he would ask me to go out to the fire escape again. But he didn't ask me again.

After that night I knew I was in love with him. I called it that to myself, and I thought about him all the time, at school and playing games in the afternoon. I used to watch every night after supper for his car to come around the corner and up to the house. I used to sing his name to myself to a tune that was popular that year, and feel like crying. I used to wait until I had gone to bed to think about what it had been like when he kissed me.

He came to see me only two or three times, quite far apart, after the holiday dance. Each time we went to the movies and he held my hand and I looked at him through the movie and thought how terribly I loved him and how beautiful he was. Then we would come home with the other boy who was along, and drink chocolate and sit in front of the fire and I would not be able to talk. He never kissed me again after the holiday dance.

After those two or three times he stopped coming to see me. I can't remember how I felt when I was hoping all the time that he would come, except that every night I used to sit at the window in my dark room after supper and wait to see if his car with the four headlights would come up around the turn. I would wait, and all the cars would go by, and then I would count a hundred slowly and make myself believe that his car would come before I got to a hundred. But it never came any more. Other boys used to come, but I can't remember anything about them.

And I remember one night later on that spring. It must have been late April by then. The frogs were singing in the swamp out behind the house, and I went out in the garden after supper and walked down through the spring twilight toward the swamp, and listened to that sweet, shrill sawing of the frogs. I knew Dave Page wouldn't come to see me any more; I suddenly knew it, although I couldn't believe it before that night.

Then I went into the house again. I was tired and I wanted to go to bed early, and I got undressed and ran a hot bath. I got into the bathtub and lay in the hot water thinking about how much I loved Dave Page and that nobody would ever kiss me like that again, even when I grew up. I remember crying in the bathtub. I hadn't cried before. I felt cold and miserable, and I couldn't stop crying. I turned more hot water on into the bath and lay there, and the heat made me feel better. After a while I went to bed. I don't remember ever feeling so bad about Dave Page after that night.

18

At this season, here in Virginia, I begin to see the trucks from the country driving in to town laden with cedar trees for Christmas — I have never been able to get used to the idea of cedar for a Christmas tree — and overflowing with running pine and mistletoe. And when the invitations written in red ink begin to come in for my daughter — "Judy Payne and Billy Judson invite you to come to their dance at the Lone Pine Country Club" — then, sometimes, I remember what it was like when I was a girl and went to the Holiday Dances at the Longwood Cricket Club.

I suppose I was fourteen when I first went to one. I remember sitting in the library at the Winsor School, staring out of the window at the traffic dashing noisily past through the slush on the Riverway, and just thinking of those words, *Holiday Dance,* that seemed to be hung with many-colored lights. My invitation had come, engraved on a square white card with a double column of patronesses, and it seemed an aeon before the date would roll around, although probably it was about two weeks away. I thought about the various terrific problems that the invitation raised: a new evening dress; getting invited to a dinner beforehand; how to be popular with boys. But, grave as these problems were, they were at the same time thrilling and made everything inside me tie into an excited knot. I can feel it now.

As far as I remember, the evening-dress problem and the dinner-party problem always got straightened out all right by the time of the dance. I think I went, in all, for three years to the Holiday Dances, so they are probably somewhat mixed in my memory, but it doesn't matter, for the feeling was always the same in those early years — high, brand-new, and as clear and hard as the frozen drifts of snow that covered the country as we drove through it in the dark on the way to the dances.

The most fun was to be spending the night with another girl, so that you went together and had someone to talk to on your return at one o'clock. I used sometimes, during the years of going to dances, to spend the night with a classmate named Mary Ellen Barksdale and called Barksy for short. Barksy was in violent revolt against her family — the whole family, not just her father and mother. She was a sort of safety valve for the rest of our class; she expressed the rebellion we could not always put into words, or felt guilty about. I can see her standing in the middle of the gym her family had outfitted over their large garage, dressed in middy and bloomers, red in the face, shaking her fists. "My mother wants to bring me up by absolutely Victorian standards! And my father just backs her up in *frustrating* me!" "Frustrating" was a word in mint condition then. I can't remember that her parents were any more frustrating than any of our parents were in those days; they all viewed with disapproval such things as possible hip flasks on boys and our going unchaperoned to dances and sitting up after midnight. What was different was how mad Barksy could get about it. She got just as mad about her older sisters. "They get everything and I don't get anything! Do you know that my sister Janet has a dress from *Paris!* They can do literally everything they want!" she would cry, and, turning, she would swing herself in pure fury up onto the trapeze bar and hang down so that her red hair fell below her head.

On the afternoon of the Holiday Dance, after school had been closed for the Christmas vacation, I would go to spend the night with Barksy in her huge, châteaulike, brownstone house out in Brookline. From the moment of arrival everything was exciting, different, not like ordinary school-term nights spent with another girl. At the top of the broad staircase, where the butler had carried my bag, Barksy met me, her eyes shining. "I've got a new dress," she announced. "It's horrible, of course; my sisters always get the best things. Come and see." The dress was laid out on her bed: pale-blue crepe romaine beaded at the waistline — which meant the hipline — with crystal bugles. We stood and stared, the breath really a bit knocked out of us by those bugles and the way the light made them sparkle. Then I recovered myself enough to open my bag in the guest room, where it had been put, and take out my own new dress and spread it on the bed. It was pink — pink taffeta with rounded panels to the skirt and a big silver tinsel rose on one hip. Robes-de-style they used to be called in those days, and it was my first. We stared at it next. *There was silver tinsel edging the panels.*

Barksy brought her dress into my room, so that we could get ready together. Then we separated to take baths. The baths we used to take in those days! Boiling hot, and counted on to accomplish all sorts of magic peripheral to cleanliness: make one's hair curl; make one's complexion — we were always talking about "complexions" — glow; get rid of blackheads; assist in reducing; and more. We met again in the guest room after steaming, and put on the underpinnings to our evening dresses, which consisted of a small bandeau and a garment called a teddy — combination chemise and drawers — tonight of some unwontedly sheer fabric, like georgette. We combed our shingled bobs and made up, which meant a dab of pale-pink powder on the nose itself, and a little lipstick, rubbed critically afterward until there was not much left. We then squirmed into our knee-length dresses, and turned to stare at each other. I don't think we said much. We were too impressed.

We descended to the drawing room, for tonight the

Barksdales were giving Barksy a dinner party — "One horrible little dinner with only six boys. My sisters get *all* the dinner parties . . ." Dinner parties were an invaluable institution; they provided a way of getting to the dance without the humiliation of being taken by a maid or, even lower, one's father or mother; they meant that here were six, or eight, or ten boys who *had* to dance with you during the evening or be rude to their dinner hostess. For ahead of us loomed the real problem, the poser: How were we to accomplish that mystery, popularity with boys? On the one hand was the horror of "getting stuck" — dancing round and round with the same boy — and there was the myth of boys who held out a dollar bill behind the girl's back to the stag line; on the other was the mortification, the defeat, of retiring to the ladies' dressing room to await the strains of "Good Night, Ladies." No wonder we were excited. We *had* to be popular, and at that age we had no idea of how to go about it. All you could do was pick up bits of folklore on the subject, and watch what the popular girls did.

The boys came to the dinner party, some in dark-blue suits, some having graduated to the maturity of a tuc. I wonder how they really looked. At the time I thought they looked important and mysterious, but then, my idea of a really fascinating older man was a Harvard freshman. We waited in the drawing room only long enough for all the guests to arrive — our schoolmates looking unfamiliar in red velvet, blue chiffon, and that degrading fabric, white tulle — for nothing, naturally, was served to us before dinner. We made conversation, of which I remember only such phrases as "Snappy like a rubber duck," "Charleston, hey, hey," and "So's your old man." We then went in to dinner, in the long, oak-paneled dining room, where, at the seventeenth-century refectory table, we were served with some such delicacy as squab. I remember the squab because one of the girls pushed too hard in cutting and the squab skimmed off her plate and across the room. The butler brought her another one. I don't think anybody laughed; we were all too near the nursery to be any too sure *we* would not make *gaffes* — perhaps even spill on our dresses.

What did we do, what could we have talked about, until it was time to go to the dance? Of course, the dance *began* at nine, and ended, except for whatever encores could be squeezed out of the orchestra, at twelve. But an end to the dance was a million light-years away from us as we drove, I in Barksy's family's car with two other girls and three boys, toward Chestnut Hill and the Cricket Club. That was, perhaps, the high moment of anticipation, with the deep snow all around under the occasional street lights, the bitter cold, the frozen, rutted roads in which the car lurched from side to side, and a broken link in the chains of a passing car going clack-clack-clack all the way into the distance.

There lies the Cricket Club, lighted up like a ship riding low and blazing from all decks. We are there, we get out, in our galoshes — with all the will to glamour in the world, we never went anywhere in winter without galoshes — and, if we are very lucky, our white bunny-fur jackets; these represented the ultimate in sophisticated outer wear for evening at the age of which I am speaking. The less lucky wear their mothers' black velvet evening wraps with the white satin lining; the even less lucky, their best day coats; the really unfortunate, those unable to fight back, the family Chinese robe, over a sweater for warmth.

And now we are face to face with it, the great test. The orchestra (most of us have picked *that* up; last year, in our infantile inexperience, we might have said "band") is playing "Nothing Could Be Finer Than to Be in Carolina in the Morning." We crowd into the ladies' dressing room, fiddle with lipsticks, busy ourselves with the disposition of coats, peer importantly into the mirror at our noses — but there is no escape, sooner or later we must enter the ballroom. Some slouch in; some saunter, with feigned indifference; others chatter madly — the peppy approach — to the boy on whose arm they enter, as they approach the row of patronesses. All let their eyes fall with relief on the red satin ribbons that some twenty of the boys are wearing across their shirt fronts; for the ribbons mark these boys as ushers, and the ushering system is Boston's great contribution to the relief of suffering girlhood.

At a private dance, the men at the hostess's dinner party beforehand became ushers automatically, and wore a carnation in their buttonholes as a badge; but private dances still lay before us and carnations were beyond our ken; red ribbons were all we knew and all we needed to know. The ushering system meant that girls were taken up and presented to the hostesses; that they were started off dancing; that a boy in the stag line who wanted to meet some girl could ask for an introduction; that a girl would not dance too long with one boy, for an usher would bring up relief. (Of course, the fear was that even the ushers might come to consider your case hopeless.) I can't imagine what the girls of other cities ever did without the ushering system.

Somehow, for me, the miracle always happened. I always had a wonderful time. It was as if, after the first few chill moments, the icicle inside, lack of confidence, were melted away by all the wonderful lights, the kaleidoscopic shifting of dancers in lovely colors, the music ("I Wonder Where My Baby Is Tonight"); so all that remained was the quivering, delightful awareness of everything outside, and no awareness of anything inside at all. A party! It always happened.

In a few years I would become scornfully critical of pink taffeta and prep-school boys, when I was a debutante and sure of having a good time, but in those days I was totally uncritical. It was as if the unsureness were a sort of required preliminary to perfect happiness. I saw nothing the matter with anything; Middlesex, Milton, St. Mark's were wonderful and ultimate places for boys to be going, the conventional lighted Christmas trees that adorned the ballroom at the Cricket Club were the last word in decoration, supper (a slice of Neapolitan ice cream) was delicious, and everything seemed as good as I had anticipated, or better.

I stood among the couples that clapped at the edge of the orchestra for more encores at the end ("Nola," "Twelfth Street Rag"); I became involved in long intense conversations in the hallway near the door, where we lingered in our galoshes and bunny fur, the boys in their fathers' coonskin coats ("When am I going to see you again?"); and, holding in my hand trophies, five red satin ushers' ribbons, I sat back all the way home in the car with Barksy behind the chauffeur in a daze of enchantment. It took us an hour to quiet down enough to go to bed; we drank the hot cocoa left out for us in a Thermos, and compared notes. ("Did you meet that divine, sort of sinister boy?" "I saw you giving Porchy Sturgis one of those searing *looks*." "He was much older. Nearly nineteen.") But finally we lay back in the twin beds in the guest room, with the windows wide to the icy night, and were instantly struck down by sleep.

We dreamed of innocent things — taffeta dresses, and boys with divine, sinister, if rather pink, faces, and flashing ushers' ribbons, and the whirl of dancers reflected in a round, shining, red, Christmas-tree ornament. And in the morning we woke, about ten, as fresh as daisies and hungry for breakfast; it felt very sophisticated to be eating breakfast off a tray, late.

Nothing is a bit like that today, at least not where I live. Here in the South they have such curious ways of celebrating Christmas; fireworks on Christmas Eve is not my idea of the holiday spirit. My daughter goes to the dances out at the Lone Pine Country Club, where there is not even any stag line, no cutting in at all; for her age group, which is about fifteen, they have a thing called a dance director, who calls figures, like in a Paul Jones, except that the whole dance is that way. It can't be any fun. The girls go to these dances unchaperoned, with boys; of course, I insist that my daughter at least go with another couple. But I worry about her; I worry about what they do in those cars out there in the dark, and about those boys driving at night, around some of the fearful mountain curves. I tell my daughter to tell the boy that's driving to be careful. But she won't listen to me. In fact, sometimes she gets furious.

My daughter seems to have a good time. She is supposed to come and tell me when she gets in, and she always says, with her voice going up to a squeal, "I had the most wonderful time I ever *had!*" Poor child, I suppose it seems so; she has no discrimination at all.

19

When i was a young girl, one of the more intense questions we would exchange as we crouched on
twin beds, spending the night with one another after
dancing all evening in the dangerous and fascinating
company of Harvard boys, was, "Do you think clothes
are important?"

The question was more soul-shaking than it might
have seemed in other, worldly-wiser cities. For behind
us stretched generations of determinedly high thinking
and plain living; around us stretched blocks of Boston
shops, filled with low-heeled sensible Oxfords, good
tweed suits guaranteed to improve with age, and the
taffeta dance dresses trimmed with tinsel roses that
were thought suitable for young girls. It was with a sense
of daring that I, in cotton-crepe pajamas and flowered
quilted dressing gown, would reply, "Yes."

Clothes had early taken on one sort of significance for
me. As a little girl my classmates at school, children of
commuting bankers, brokers, and businessmen, were
dressed in striped chambray or checked gingham, the

belts worn low around the hips. For dancing school, on late, snow-muffled winter afternoons, they wore white embroidered muslin with pink or blue taffeta sashes.

I, alas, was not dressed similarly. My mother had what I now realize was a more sophisticated taste in children's clothes. For school I wore little short linen dresses in gray or tan, with their corded waists up under my armpits. They must have been charming, but I wanted to die; my clothes were wrong. What I wore for dancing school conformed even less to local fashion: black velveteen, very straight and short, with a gold moire sash run through slots at a high waistline; or the same dress in brown velveteen with a Roman-stripe sash. With these, I wore black patent-leather ankle-tie slippers with the straps coming from behind the ankle to button in front; even this was wrong, for the others wore slippers whose straps came from one side to cross the instep to the other side. For a number of years I experienced the full horror of being the black sheep in a white pack.

Then, for some parental reason I have never fathomed, my luck changed. It was summer, and I was invited to visit at the seashore in Rhode Island for a fortnight. I was not especially elated, for I never had a good time anywhere; my face, I can see in photographs of that period, was set in an expression of gloom. My mother said, "You haven't got anything to wear. We must go to Jordan Marsh's and buy you some dresses." Buy dresses? Us? My clothes had always been made for me at home.

I can remember the dresses we bought as clearly as if they hung in my closet today. They will not sound like much. One was a brown-and-white checked gingham with a narrow sash of the same material. One was a black-and-white pin-checked gingham with a broad white organdy collar. The third was orange Shantung, to wear for dinner. But they changed my life.

It might be instructive to consider why my visit turned out to be a dream of bliss — sailing, participating in three-legged races, playing beanbags in the evening, taking long, happy walks through the rhododendron- and laurel-bordered paths of the South County woods. The dresses I wore for these occasions could not have been anything exceptional. They were certainly less exceptional than my dresses that originated at home. But they had originated in the world — they were world dresses; in them I felt I, too, could live in the world as if I belonged there.

Of course, at the bottom of this illusion that clothes make the child lay the comparative system of values which so haunts the minds of the young: my mother is prettier than your mother; our house is bigger than your house; my father is stronger than your father. But also, disastrously, it can run: your house is nicer than our house; your father is richer than my father; your clothes are better than my clothes.

Later, in my teens, when I was going to the Winsor School in Boston, such a hierarchy of values still obtained. High on the list of perfections stood Fair Isle and Shetland knit sweaters. Why were they considered so perfect? They just were. Accordion-pleated dark-blue or dark-green skirts came close. Plaid wool skirts were on the list. The sweater-and-skirt costume, its sweater worn over a white cotton blouse with a round collar, was an absolute safe-conduct to acceptability in that school which had no uniform. The girls who wore dresses never looked right; and the more dressy the dress, the wronger.

Those were the years when we first began going to dances. No tongue can tell the edge-of-a-precipice tension of the moment when we faced a Holiday Dance or the subscription dances held at Eliot Hall or Brattle Hall. Touchingly innocuous as those parties must have been, with their fruit punch, their barrage of patronesses, their pink-cheeked Milton or Middlesex seniors for partners, to us they might as well have been the Court of St. James's, only more sinister. In a sense it was as if we faced some appalling test of our own quality (and in this, I suppose, lay the peril of the system). Our future lives seemed to hang in the balance. Naturally, enormous care had to be exercised in the selection of suitable garments in which to deck ourselves for such a rite. I see my own first real dance dress now, made of orange chiffon, the top bloused over its tinsel girdle; the skirt, made of a dozen orange chiffon handkerchiefs, fell in many points to break the line of a knee-length hem; the neck was bateau. Upon it I pinned my tremulous hopes.

I was not confounded. From the first I had a marvelous time at the dances. As those school years passed and we graduated to older dances, to the Friday Evenings at the Somerset, the private dances for subdebutantes in people's houses or at the Brookline Country Club, clothes took on an increasingly burning significance. Certain dresses had a cosmic importance in my wardrobe. There were dresses in which I always had a good time and those dresses, as smart or smarter, which seemed to possess no magic. It was almost as if one were incapable of assuming the responsibility for one's own popularity or lack of it, and dumped it, instead, upon a dress, or a pair of silver slippers, or a particular string of fake pearls, worn looped once around a thin, immature throat and then left hanging almost to the waist.

I remember a lavender chiffon dress in which I achieved my own stag line in a corner of the small ballroom at the Somerset; why this should have happened seems curious, since the knee-length hem of the dress was bordered with lavender ostrich feathers which came off on the knees of the boys' black trousers, so that you could tell which boys I had been dancing with. I remember another successful dress, short, tubular, made of coarse cream-colored lace over a scarlet slip, which burst into a flounce of lace ruffles over the knees.

But I remember just as well a dress made of raspberry crepe, embroidered with dozens of little bouquets of flowers in pink and silver beads, which we bought on a trip to New York. It was far smarter than any other dress I owned, but I never had the time in it that I did in my luck-shot dresses. I remember a mauve taffeta robe-de-style, from Hickson's on Boylston Street, with curved petallike panels lapping over each other on the bouffant skirt. It must have been charming, and my father wanted to paint me in it, but for some occult reason it did not work; I dreaded wearing it and for the most part it hung in my closet.

Some of my most treasured costumes must have been appalling. I remember a purple crepe dress in which I used to go tea-dancing at Shepard's Colonial, and with which I would wear a purple felt cloche and purple gloves. The inspiration for this arrangement had been a tale a Boston boy had told me on his return, eyes bunging out, from holidays spent in New York — of a rapturously popular girl, one of those legends of popularity which each of the Eastern cities boasted one or more of, who never wore anything but purple. She had purple eyes, he added, gasping slightly. I didn't have purple eyes, but I wanted to be a legend myself, so shortly afterward I assembled this purple concoction. I must say I never had any complaints about it from the audience for whom it was intended; but memory reels.

Then we were upon the year toward which everything had been converging — the year of coming out.

If clothes had been important, they were of world-shattering significance now. They were something to brood over; to go especially to New York for; to bully one's parents, kindly but firmly, into letting one select according to one's very definite ideas as to what would and what would not succeed, especially on the dance floor. The older generation had such a depressing predilection for white taffeta and tulle, whereas all the debutantes I knew were convinced that black, and preferably black satin, was what was needed to bring them the triumphs they longed for. But to a girl they all came out in white — white tulle, white taffeta, white brocade, nothing but ghastly old white. The boys shared our aversion to this pristine color. "She looked all right — horribly pure, of course," they would say of some wretched girl on her great night, or, "Boston girls are so darn unsophisticated. The best thing in Boston," they would always continue in lordly tones, "is the Merchants Limited leaving for New York." We would humbly agree, convinced that in New York the girls were paragons of sophistication and wonderful, acceptable impurity.

Therefore it behooved one not to spare the lash in extracting something black out of one's parents — if not the coming-out dress, then a subsidiary evening dress, or if they still held the line of sheer stuffiness, at least a black dress for tea-dancing. Some poor unfortunates remained restricted to girlish colors — "girlish" was the most contemptuous adjective one could use — throughout their whole year, but most of us managed at least one black costume, in which we sat, eyes narrowed, looking mysterious — or so we devoutly hoped. I remember my own black achievement — not much of an achievement, really, since it had a boring fold of pink at the neck; but otherwise it was all black, black georgette, with a rhinestone buckle at its hipline waist. In it I can recall tea-dancing with a very smooth Harvard senior who thrust his chin far forward as he danced, snakily, to the strains of "Who," played by Billy Lossez's orchestra.

If, in those days, New York was our mecca, Garbo was our ideal. We sat through her movies three or four times in order to study her every gesture. The more daring among us wore our short hair straight, like hers; pulled a felt riding hat down recklessly over one eye; slouched along with our hands deep in our pockets. It was considered intriguing to stare in silence at somebody who had asked a question, until at last one said, "I dawn't knaw," in a Swedish accent.

Our lives were turned topsy-turvy, then, when Garbo wore a long dress in one of her movies — I don't remember which, perhaps *Flesh and the Devil*. All at once a canker of dissatisfaction ate at us: short dresses no longer seemed the chic desideratum they had been. But there was nothing to do about it. Boston shops had never heard of such a thing as a long dress. We could only yearn, and murmur, "I want to be alawn."

"You look very nice," my mother said with moderation, as I prepared to go out to dinner one night in a pale-green chiffon dress with crystal beading around the hips.

"This awful old thing?" I responded automatically. "It's so dowdy and short."

"Would you like a long dress?" my mother asked in mild astonishment. "We could have one made at home, you know."

I stared at her. "Could I have black?"

"Velvet," she qualified, nodding.

And that was the genesis of my dress that looked like Garbo's. Of black chiffon velvet, it came slightly below the knees in front — but that looked long, then — and in the back it came down to the floor. It was cut in a low V, filled in with lace over pink chiffon, and its waist was at my natural waistline, whence the skirt fell away in long folds. I wore it first to a dance at the Somerset.

I don't remember, specifically, the time I had that night, but it must have been all right. A year ago I was visiting in Washington and was introduced to a woman of my own middle-aged generation who said, when she heard my maiden name, "Oh, you're the girl who wore the long black dress in Boston."

As I laughed, I was thinking not so much of the Somerset as of dancing school, long ago, when I used to wear black velveteen made at home, so different from the others, and was all wrong.

20

JINNY WELCH AND I WERE EIGHTEEN THE WINTER WE both came out in Boston. We had been separated by boarding schools, summer camps, and trips abroad for several years, but now the two of us, best friends throughout a country childhood across the street from each other, met again daily with all the old affinity. We must have been a pair of remarkably silly girls; we were drunk with the wine of youth and we could not stop laughing.

"I went to the most hysterical tea at the Victoria today," Jinny would perhaps tell me as we dressed together for a dinner dance. The words popped from her lips as though they were too preposterous to contain. "There were thirty Boston girls with tried and true ankles, and the hostess was wearing health shoes and a hat trimmed with canned tomatoes."

My eyes met hers in a kind of ecstasy. When we could speak again for laughing, I asked, "Do you suppose Greetings will be at the dance?"

Greetings was the name that Jinny had bestowed upon a moonfaced, pudgy Harvard boy who, when cutting in, would clasp one's hand in his soft, wet one and gravely remark, "Greetings." We had long ago, and with rapture, forgotten what his real name was. If at a party I saw Jinny, or she me, revolving in the arms of Greetings, we would exchange one wild glance and go off into gales. "Beg pardon?" Greetings would inquire.

Part of our silliness was due to the overwhelming new sense of freedom that attended coming out. After years of the compulsions of school, suddenly one could get up late, take nothing but orange juice and coffee for breakfast, spend time before the glass experimenting with lipstick and eyeshadow, and wander over to meet at the Welches' garage and drive to town for a shopping trip or a debutante luncheon. A small Plymouth sedan had been set aside for Jinny's exclusive use; the very word Plymouth had assumed for us an extravagant, reckless sound.

The world of our country childhood was left behind, populated now only by May, Jinny's younger sister — a mere sixteen-year-old who went to the Country Day School — and by my painter parents, whose idea of hell was to have to go to some major debutante ball. The Welch boys were both in Harvard, and we saw them at the dances. Their father, Mr. Thompson Welch, continued to conduct his mysterious, cosmopolitan, lawyer's, widower's life from the apartment in Bos-

208

ton whence he had for years dispensed a peculiarly severe and repressive discipline to the house in the country, a governess being still deputed to carry out his commands and to chaperon the girls.

Jinny and I now belonged to the great world, or what passed for the great world to our bedazzled eyes. Perhaps we would dive into the Boston subway and let whim decide what car we took. "Lechmere!" Jinny exclaimed on one such occasion. "Let's go to hysterical old Lechmere, where the lechers come from." Gasping, we leaped aboard just as the doors slid shut. As is the case with most Boston subway trains, it shortly came out into the light of day. Jinny's nose was pressed to the pane of her window; her enormous dark eyes took in everything we passed. "Six Little Tailors!" she cried. "See the sign?"

Our eyes met. "Let's get off," I said.

We ran down the Elevated's steps into the narrow downtown-Boston street, and then up four dark flights to a loft. Jinny opened the door upon a workroom full of people. "We wanted to see the Six Little Tailors tailoring," she said in a strangled voice. "Vat vas dot?" asked a middle-aged, bald man in a singlet. We could not control ourselves longer. As we ran down the four flights again, we burst into peals of inextinguishable laughter.

We thought it terribly funny to call ourselves the McMuffin sisters, Pansy and Myrtle. We thought it terribly funny, one afternoon when the McMuffins were holding a cocktail party at my father's studio in Boston and we found we must order ice, that we did not know what amount of ice to order.

"We don't actually need very much," Jinny explained earnestly, having got the ice company on the phone. "Well, *how* much, lady?" I heard the man's patient voice say. Jinny threw me a wild glance. "Five pounds?" she suggested over the wire. "Lady," the man's voice said, "if I sent you five pounds, it wouldn't get there." After she had settled for twenty-five pounds, Jinny hung up and we dissolved into giggles. It made a wonderful story with which, later, to convulse the Harvard seniors who came to the party; the extravagance of Jinny's language in telling it was much admired.

On very late nights, after we had gone to two or possibly even more dances, we slept in town; our parents did not think it suitable that we should drive home to the country, with boys or without them. We could stay at Mr. Welch's apartment, where Jinny, by fixing Waterhouse, Mr. Welch's valet, with her large, what she called stewed-prune eyes, would persuade him to bring us a cocktail apiece while we were dressing. Or we could stay at my father's studio. On such nights my father slept downstairs on a day bed in the studio itself. Upstairs, opening off the balcony, was a tiny sitting room and an even tinier bedroom, which had been charmingly arranged by my mother as a *pied-à-terre* where I could change my clothes between engagements, dress for the evening, sleep after balls, and entertain a few friends.

Jinny and I would hold post-mortems in the small hours after an evening's triumphs. Jinny, in a knee-length sheath of gold sequins like a shining coat of mail, from which her sleek dark head, like a boy's, rose on its lovely long neck, would light a last cigarette in a long green holder. "The most hysterical man kept cutting in," she would say. "He had a pig on his watch chain, and he looked like a pig, so I said, 'I beg your pardon, but by any possible chance could you be a member of the Porcellian Club?' and he said, 'How did you know?' "

"Jinny!" I moaned, and we collapsed into our eternal laughter.

When we went to bed, it was on the cot in the little bedroom. I don't think Mr. Welch ever realized that there was, at the studio, only one bed for us to sleep in; and when we insisted vehemently to my father that we *preferred* sharing a bed, he seemed baffled but convinced. The one who slept on the outer side of the cot had to hold herself in bed all night by propping one hand on the floor; it is a measure of our vitality that we found this inexpressibly funny.

We would arise at noon or later, thoroughly refreshed, and bathe, dress, and breakfast. Perhaps we might then drive to the country in the Plymouth to see what was going on out there. May Welch would often have got home from afternoon sports at school by the time we strode into the Welches' house from our sophisticated adventures in the metropolis — both tall, thin as laths, wearing high-heeled shoes and knee-length beige dresses and helmet hats and Chanel pearls, and laughing our heads off.

May always had been and still was plump. She had soft brown hair and Jinny's brown eyes, but without the snap in them. Her obvious worship of us was agreeable, and we would allow her to do her homework in the living room with us while we chattered away in the argot we used, with its incredulous tone. Although Miss Perkins, the governess, could not bring herself to countenance alcoholic drinks for young girls, on a couple of occasions when she had a day off and we were spending a quiet evening in the country for a change we made cocktails and let May take a thrilled sip off the top of one.

We were sitting thus, playing "Do-Do-Do" on the gramaphone in the living room of the Welches' historic house — with its big oval braided rug, Early American pine furniture, and ship prints — when the telephone rang in the dark old hall beyond and Jinny went to answer it. In a minute she called to me, "It's Albo Cartright. He wishes to inquire what the McMuffin sisters are planning over the week end."

I joined Jinny at the telephone and we took turns talking to Albo and his Harvard roommate, punctuating our jargon with bursts of mirth. When we finally hung up, we went on sitting out in the hall, Jinny in the telephone chair and I on the rag rug at her feet. "So then I went into an absolutely searing silence," Jinny recounted, of some contretemps with Albo's roommate. "I could see him thinking how mysterious and uncommunicative I am." I caught her eye and we went into gales.

It was quite a time before either of us noticed that the needle of the Victrola in the living room was stuck in a groove of "Do-Do-Do." "Heart begins to sigh, heart begins to sigh, heart begins to sigh, heart . . ." sang the high, sweet voice over and over and over.

Simultaneously we jumped up and went back into the living room. May Welch was lying on the floor with her eyes closed, breathing heavily. The gin bottle we had made our Martini from, which had been nearly half full, was empty.

My eyes met Jinny's above May's prostrate body. Jinny was not looking sophisticated any more. She was looking about twelve, and terrified.

"We've got to do something quick," she said. "Suppose Father finds out."

After a childhood spent with Mr. Welch looming in the background I could appreciate the validity of her fear. Mr. Welch was not a man to ask for or to supply explanations. He merely dealt out retribution with a cold, relentless, legal hand. When Royal Welch flunked fifth-form Latin, he had his allowance suspended for six months, without more ado.

I delved into my memory for novels I had read, in search of recipes for treating people who had passed out. "Perhaps we should pour cold water on her face," I suggested.

"We'll put her in a cold shower," Jinny declared. "That's what they do with drunks. Come on, you take her feet and I'll take her shoulders."

But May weighed about a hundred and fifty pounds, and her satin-smooth skin was, moreover, extremely slippery. In the end we more dragged than carried her across the living room, down the step into the hall, and into the downstairs bathroom. We tumbled her into the tub, where she lay still, breathing loudly.

We stood back, breathing rather loudly ourselves.

"Do you think we should turn the shower onto her?" I asked doubtfully; it seemed a heartless thing to do to a helpless person. "Maybe we could just run the water into the tub."

"That does sound less of a shock," Jinny agreed.

We set to work to undress May, realizing too late that we should have done it before. After considerable pulling, yanking, and tipping her from side to side, we succeeded, with the exception of May's elastic girdle, which we were unable to pry off her plump hips. Then we turned on the cold water and stood watching as the tub gradually filled.

"I think she's supposed to come to with a jerk," Jinny said hopefully.

But May did not come to at all. Jinny looked help-lessly at me and I looked helplessly back, while beside us May lay senseless in the cold water. She was not breathing so loudly now.

"Maybe we'd better let the water out again," I said. "It's rather a cold day."

So we let the water out again. We endeavored to get May out of the tub to dry her, but that was impossible. Her body was cold, and as smooth and slippery as rubber. Suddenly we both realized that the whole matter had got way beyond us. "What's that d-d-doctor's name your family has?" Jinny asked, stammering as she always did when she was nervous. "I d-d-don't want to call our d-d-doctor. He'd tell Father."

So I rang up dear old Dr. Stephenson, who had taken care of me through tonsillitis and bronchitis and chicken pox. I explained what had happened to May Welch and where she was now.

"I'll be right along," Dr. Stephenson interrupted.

"We thought a cold bath was the right thing for drunk people," I began defensively.

"That's when they're conscious," he said, and hung up.

In a few minutes he was with us — little, pink, bus-tling, and white-mustached. He lost no time. "Got to get her right into bed," he explained, as he cut May's girdle off with scissors. By means of a sheet slipped un-der her body, the three of us lifted her out of the tub and onto a straight chair, in which we carried her into the downstairs guest room and put her on the bed.

"Get another blanket — two blankets," Dr. Stephenson directed, sitting on the edge of the bed and listening to May's heart. We wrapped her naked body in the two blankets and drew the sheet up over her, and covered her all up with several quilts. Dr. Stephenson took a hypodermic syringe from his bag and filled it.

He stayed with her an hour more. Then he came out into the hall. "She's sleeping naturally," he said to us. "I think she'll be all right now. She's got a strong heart." He paused and viewed us. "Never, *never* put an unconscious person into cold water."

We shook our heads obediently.

"I'll call back in the morning to see how she is," he said. "Keep her warm in bed. Call me if anything seems wrong."

Jinny coughed.

"Listen, Dr. Stephenson," she said rapidly. "I know I'm horrible, but do you mind — I mean, Father would simply die if he knew about this. Couldn't you make up something else to be what happened to May, so he won't have to know about the gin? I mean, I'm responsible, and I'll probably be sent to Mesopotamia or the Ruhr or somewhere if he finds out."

The doctor took a long time looking her up and down. "All right," he said at last. "We'll call it food poisoning."

He glanced from one of us to the other, twitched his

216

mustache from side to side, and departed. I think he had satisfied himself that we had learned a good lesson and were thoroughly scared.

He was right. We were. It was a full minute before Jinny turned her enormous eyes upon me. Gradually they began to sparkle. "How absolutely luridly fantastic," she began.

What had happened was our secret. But Jinny had never been any good at keeping secrets, even when it was to her advantage to do so. Around two o'clock in the morning, about a week later, I walked into one of the small sitting-out rooms at the Copley Plaza on the arm of a beau, in the course of a large ball given by some Chestnut Hill people for their rawboned daughter. There was Jinny, in the center of one of those circles she always attracted, wearing an orange velvet dress and agitating a large orange ostrich-feather fan. From across the room I could see her eyes dancing and hear her excited little laugh. As I approached, I heard her say in those swift, incredulous accents, ". . . so we had to drag her across the entire house like a great sack of petrified potatoes, her head going bump, bump, bump at every step."

My heart sank. It might sound very funny at that hour of the night among friends, but I had begun to realize that any story that amuses its listeners tends to get around. What would happen when it reached Mr.

Welch, seated at ease in one of his clubs, that his younger daughter had drunk half a bottle of gin and passed out?

I tried to catch Jinny's eye to shake my head at her. But now that she was out from under the shadow of fear of her father, she was wearing her wildest, most uncontrollable expression.

"There lay that vast girlish lump, out like a light after the merest taste of gin," she was saying. "So we turned on the cold water in the tub and hoped for the best. But she remained dead to the world, while around her the icy waters steadily r—" Jinny stopped.

Over her mobile, sparkling face came an extraordinary change, a look of utter astonishment and consternation. She continued in a different voice, "Actually we might have killed her."

Some one of her audience, still keyed up to Jinny's storytelling pitch, emitted a small, nervous giggle. Jinny turned and stared thoughtfully at him.

"I don't believe it's funny," she said.

After an uncomfortable pause, everyone was only too glad when Jinny took off on another and this time hilarious story — something about getting the Plymouth stuck in a snowbank on the way to town, and how, out from a house, had come to help her "a hysterical, germ-laden little man in high button boots and plush fours." The words seemed to pop from her lips, and tears of laughter stood in her eyes.

As usual when she was in top form, she had her audience with her; and within a week I was meeting people who were using the phrase "plush fours" to be funny.

21

THE FIRST OF THESE EXPERIENCES THAT I HAVE LATELY
begun to *notice*, or at least the first I can remember,
happened when I was a child. I was shy as a child, and
I believed in my shyness; that is to say, it never occurred
to me that our town was not really inhabited exclusively
by stern, haughty people — ladies with heads held erect
on scrawny necks, gentlemen who guffawed at one's
timid remarks, children whose joy it was by word and
bullying deed to make one feel even more of a worm
than one did already.

This view of my home town was not diminished by
the remarks of my Irish nurse, an old woman who had
been with me since I was born. "Them," she would say
about the people of the town, "with their fine houses
and their crool tongues." She even spoke disparagingly
of the tradespeople in the village. "Will you look at the
bad face on that Muldoon," she would whisper as we
passed the newsstand on our way to the drugstore to
buy soda for Nana's wind. "It's the Black Irish in him

coming out." After that, how could I doubt that the old newsdealer was an ogre? "Oh, it's a hard town and a terrible time," she would sigh over the cup of tea that had been boiling on the stove all the time we had been away on our walk. "There's many with hearts of stone and few with a kind word. I'll tell you, my mind goes back to Whale Harbor, where matters were very different. It was 'Nana, would it be too much trouble?' and 'Miss Hagerty, will you be wanting to go to the early Mass?' and all the time the sun shining, and the sea sparkling, and the flowers popping out into bloom all over the grass. Will I make you a cup of Cambridge tea now?"

She meant cambric tea, and she knew I would want it, to sip while she began to tell me one of her long, rambling, beautiful stories of Whale Harbor, in Maine, where she had once worked for some people named Parkinson, creatures of goodness and love, and where life in no particular resembled the dark town she and I were fated to endure.

At that age I hadn't enough geography to know exactly where Maine was; Whale Harbor was more an island, in my mind, a floating isle of bliss. On it lived an old farmer named Mr. Goodheart, who delighted to give lifts, in his blue cart behind his white horse, to persons walking along the road, all in the perpetual sunshine. At the beach, the children ran hand in hand down to the sea, and the ladies sat protecting their complexions under large beach umbrellas and small ruffled parasols. They were all beauties, and the children were full of gifts and promise. Everybody was nice to everybody else. "Sure, there wasn't enough they could do to show their kindness of heart," Nana would say. "It was luncheons here and dinners there, and faytes and festivals every day or two, never leaving out the widow and the poor orphan and the stranger in a strange land." That last was Nana, of course, and although I had a perfectly good father and mother, I felt the poor orphan was me. It made a foursquare picture of Paradise in my imagination, one that I loved to roam around in as I was going to sleep; I never expected I would see Whale Harbor with my own eyes.

But when I was twelve, and in Ferris waists, and had been without a nurse for two or three years, I was invited one day by a girl at school named Catherine Calloway to visit her at her family's summer house at Whale Harbor. That night, as I was going to sleep, my mind roamed joyfully, peacefully, along the roads, beside the ponds, and down the long white beach at Whale Harbor. I knew I would be happy there. Catherine had never seemed to me a particularly pleasant girl, but that, I was sure, was because I had known her only in this sad and forbidding place. In Whale Harbor she would be different.

According to all the books, I should have had a bitter awakening. But the point is that I did not. I spent a week in Whale Harbor, and the sun shone all day every day, the sea sparkled and was kind as we ran down to it hand in hand through the soft sand. One day near noon, as we were walking to the beach in our striped gingham dresses and sneakers, and the sun threatened to become a touch hotter than the sun may get in Paradise, there was the rumble of cart wheels behind us, and a moment later a Yankee voice called down, "Where ye bound for?"

"The beach!" we cried.

"Climb aboard," the old man called cheerfully, and we clambered up over the dusty wheel to the high, high seat of the blue cart. "Git up, there — what ye 'baout?" he said to his horse, and we rumbled off bumpily down the long white road.

"Thank you, Mr. Goodheart," Catherine said when we got down where the beach road branched off. I was not surprised. Of course he was the original Mr. Goodheart; of course the ladies disposed upon the beach and on the little weathered porch of the bathhouse were as beautiful as flowers; I had always known that this was the way it would be, and it was. Fetes and festivals were given every day or two, just as Nana had said, and everybody was lovely to me; at "church," held Sundays in the house of the owner of the largest place at Whale Harbor, we all sang the hymns at the very tops of our voices — "O worship the King, All glorious above!" — and afterward everyone strolled about the grounds, the ladies with their ruffled parasols and the gentlemen in white flannel trousers, dark-blue jackets, and boater hats with club bands, and said to each other kind and complimentary things. The only sorrow was to leave this lovely place. I sat on the porch of the Calloways' hilltop house waiting for the station taxi to come and fetch me. The salt marshes stretched far away, flat and hazy, to the blue line that was the sea; the sun shone warm and yellow on everything — the sparse, late-blooming pink-and-white apple blossoms of Maine, the bayberry bushes that smelled so pungent, the sweet fern and the sassafras trees; *"Bobwhite!"* said a quail suddenly from behind a tumble-down stone wall. I was driven to the station by Mr. Easton, who owned the taxi. He was a stringy, lanky man, but full of love and goodness; he carried my bag out to the platform for me and set it down and looked at me and said, "You got everything now?" As the train came chuffing down the track, I drew in my last lungful of salt air, blue air, Whale Harbor air.

A year or two later I began going to a Boston school and knowing Boston girls. The circle of dark, forbidding faces seemed to follow me when I went, so that now it was the faces of Boston that seemed cold, haughty, unkind. A girl named Corinne Bridges and I used to talk about how mean the Boston girls were, how stiff and mocking. We would sit on the little landing at the top of the third flight of stairs, outside the door to the art studios, where the sun streamed down through a sky-light on us. "But the worst," Corinne said one day, fingering the spit curl in the middle of her forehead, "is a place called Whale Harbor. The absolute worst. Every snooty thing, every horrible Bostonian thing is absolutely a hundred per cent more so there. Mother says the social atmosphere is so cold there it never gets up above zero even in August." She patted her cootie garages. I could only stare.

The next such episode that I can remember was when I was a young woman and visiting older friends, a pair of sisters, in Connecticut. The sisters were remarkable women, and as diverse as they were remarkable. The older, my particular friend, Miss Agnes, was kind and open as the sun; she had been for many years the head-mistress of a school outside Philadelphia. The younger by a year or two, Miss Olive, was dour and moody. A talented poet, she seemed to live in a shadowy hole, from which she would pop her head out to say some-thing. A moment later she would pop it back in again. I admired her for her wit and for her writing, but there was something depressing about her presence, and I was not sorry when, during my visit, she took herself off on a trip to Boston, where she intended to bury herself in the Athenaeum for a fortnight on some sort of research project. I was happy to be alone with Miss Agnes, whom I admired extravagantly. Her courage, her firm decisiveness, her pooh-poohing of all the doubting side of life were as stimulating to me as strong drink. It was the way I had always wanted to be. We would sit at breakfast out on the little flagged terrace in the warm September sunshine and the utter peace — the nearest village was three miles away — while Miss Agnes read the day before's paper to me; the Ruhr is what I remember. She would read along in her calm, intelligent voice, and then she would put the paper down beside the toast and say, "What rubbish!" I was lost in admiration; imagine being able to say rubbish about the Ruhr!

It had to be the day of the thunderstorm, of course, that it happened. The storm had crackled and smashed around us for an hour or two in the late afternoon, and when Miss Agnes tried to telephone for a taxi for Margaret, the maid, who went home at night, she found the wire had gone dead. Miss Olive had taken the old Jordan with her when she went to Boston, and we had been depending on delivery wagons for our food and on our own two feet for anything else we needed. It was beginning to get dark when Margaret, looking as cross as if we had cut the telephone wires ourselves, started to walk home. At about half past ten, Miss Agnes had a heart attack.

We were sitting in the living room before the fire, and Miss Agnes was reading aloud to me from Nietzsche. She frowned once or twice, and I expected her to put down the book and say that *Zarathustra* was rubbish.

But, instead, she put down the book and said, "I'm having some sort of an attack. Help me to get over to the sofa, my dear. I want to lie down."

For Miss Agnes to say "lie down," for Miss Agnes to say "help me" was cataclysmic. I stared at her while the big clock out in the hall went "Tock . . . tock . . ." Then I hurried over to her and, my arms under hers, assisted her to the old sofa, with its threadbare sides. She let out a big sigh when she was lying on her back, and said, "My chest —" I knelt beside her, holding her hand and waiting for her to tell me what to do, without ever thinking this was at all odd of me. Miss Agnes always told one what to do. She did now. She said, "You might try the telephone again. But if it's still down, you'll have to walk in to Dr. Moffatt's. I have no intention of dying, and I want some help."

The clock in the hall struck eleven while I was vainly trying to get some sound out of the telephone. Dead as a piece of wood. I put my head back into the living room. "Will you be all right while I walk to the village?" I asked, and Miss Agnes said tartly, "A lot righter than if you don't go." But in a shameful way it was myself I was worrying about now. I was afraid to walk to the village in the middle of the night.

The way to the village lay up hill and down dale, between stone quarries like great drilled cavities in the contour of Connecticut; past Humdrum Farm, which was not humdrum at all but was said to be haunted — even in the daytime its empty windows stared out at one like eye sockets; past the Rainbow Gardens, a roadhouse which attracted peculiar elements from all over the township; through the Big Swamp, or one end of it, the roadbed being filled in and raised above the low-lying marshes on either hand; and so into the village.

I had always been afraid of the outdoor darkness. But now I was bitterly ashamed of my fear, in the face of Miss Agnes's need. I went into the entry to get a coat, for from the faint sound upon the windowpanes I knew it was still raining. I switched on the overhead bulb, and there, upon wooden pegs, hung my own tweed coat, Miss Agnes's and Miss Olive's knockabout coats, and a plaid woolen Inverness cape, with an old hat to match hanging with it — a cape for bad weather, which I had admired since the beginning of my visit. Sensible, efficient, yet jaunty, it looked, I thought, just like its owner; no need to ask whether this was Miss Agnes's. Besides, I had seen her wearing it in the garden on the one other rainy day we had had since my arrival.

In my childish state of nerves, my hands seemed to reach for the cape and hat of their own accord; like the Cloak of Invisibility, the cape would, I felt, confer an aura of protection upon its wearer. I felt that by wearing Miss Agnes's cape I would put on the garment of Miss Agnes's courage. I put on the cape and the hat and went out into the darkness. My heart beat fast as I stepped off down the unlighted country road into the dark. But with the cape around me I had the feeling that I *was* Miss Agnes. I was not afraid.

I drove back with Dr. Moffatt; he gave Miss Agnes a shot; he and I carried her up to her bed and made her comfortable. "I think you'll be all right now," he said, viewing her like a work of art.

"I'm sure I will," she said. Then she turned her head so that she could see me, standing in an attitude of readiness to do what I was told next. "Aren't you ever going to take Olive's coat off?" she asked.

Both these episodes occurred years ago. Events that are more recent have reminded me of them. A couple of years ago, I was moving into a new house, into a strange town, or, as the real-estate man called it, "community." I felt very shy about it, even at my age — very unsure of my own ability to make a place for myself among a lot of new people.

I went to New York to buy slip-cover and curtain material, and while I was there I was taken to a cocktail party at the apartment of a beautiful young Indian woman. It was an hour of pure enchantment. Within the square room the people moved and talked quietly, smiling, as though imbued with the serenity of our hostess. She stood talking to her guests, tall and like a figure in the Elgin marbles, with her lovely apricot-colored sari flung over one shoulder, its pleats falling from the hip to a border of heavy, intricate gold. We all drank, in a leisurely way, from widely rounded, short-stemmed goblets; we drank both whiskey and Martinis from them. This, like every detail of that beautiful party, seemed to me unique and precious; whiskey had never looked like this or tasted like this. There was something about drinking liquor from a goblet. Nobody but my hostess, I felt, could have thought of such a charming idea.

So when I had moved into my new house in that alarming-sounding "community," I bought new glasses for the parties I would give; I spent some time looking for just what I wanted — wide, rounded goblets with a low foot. I had the feeling, when I found them, that they would make my parties, and they did. People gave little exclamations of surprise and pleasure when they were handed these globular glasses filled with liquor, and it seemed as if the aura of the graceful Indian clung even to these reminders of her special way of doing things; people drank more slowly, with more enjoyment. The goblets were a success, and I did not do so badly myself.

Months later, I was in New York again and, in front of St. Patrick's Cathedral, ran into the young Indian woman. I had been told that in the daytime she wore ordinary American clothes, and in her tweed coat and brown felt hat it was hard to find the exalted, mythical creature she had seemed in a sari; she looked like a nice brunette American girl. "You must come to see me again," she said.

"I'd love to," I said. "I've never forgotten that afternoon." And I told her about how enchanting it had all seemed to me, and about how I had copied her original way of using goblets for drinks.

She laughed. "You must come and see me in my *new* apartment," she said, "now that I have my own things. The flat where you came before was sublet, and I took it furnished. I'm glad you liked the goblets, because that was all the glasses there were, and I always wondered whether people would mind."

Most recent of all these, to me, curious experiences was one I had in a plane flying to Montreal several months ago. The other participant in the experience was, this time, a stranger, an old lady. She had the seat beside me; I noticed her when we boarded the plane — a tiny, white-haired old lady with a small, strong, positive face. She might be, I thought, a Scot.

As time went by, in the air, I became increasingly nervous. The bumping was awful. We flew into a heavy snowstorm and climbed above it, but when we were up there, I could see the wing just ahead of my window beginning to ice up. I thought of taking a sedative pill I had in my bag, but just then I turned and looked at the old lady beside me, and her strong, long-lipped, indomitable profile seemed to pull me together. I felt I didn't need any pill. Every few minutes, I would turn my head and look at her, and sometimes she would look back at me and smile — a brisk sort of smile, with no nonsense about it.

I thought how remarkable it is that in this world where we are all strangers to one another a stranger can nevertheless, without a word, send new courage into one's cowering heart, just by a glance, or by not even that — simply by the cut of his jib. It was impossible to stay afraid beside my old lady — not that she was cocky or brash-looking. She had a quiet toughness, I thought, just a little lift to her chin, a lifetime's stiffness to her lip. I had the feeling that my hand was in hers, and I was not afraid.

When we were preparing to leave the plane at Montreal, I said good-by to her. I had the feeling that it would not do to say anything emotional or sentimental to this old lady, and so all I said was, "I've enjoyed sitting beside you." It seemed to me good and proper that the fear, the conquest of fear with the help of that rocky profile beside me, the confidence that had flowed from her to me should never be mentioned.

She took my hand. "And I, too, my dear," she said. "I don't know what I should have done without your courageous presence beside me. I don't mind telling you I was a bit nervy up there."